MW00379178

HOW
WOULD
GOD VOTE?

✧

ALSO BY DAVID KLINGHOFFER

The Lord Will Gather Me In: My Journey to Jewish Orthodoxy

The Discovery of God: Abraham and the Birth of Monotheism

Why the Jews Rejected Jesus: The Turning Point in Western History

Shattered Tablets: Why We Ignore the Ten Commandments at Our Peril

David Klinghoffer

HOW
WOULD
GOD VOTE?

Why the Bible
Commands You to Be a
Conservative

DOUBLEDAY

New York London Toronto Sydney Auckland

CD
DOUBLEDAY

Copyright © 2008 by David Klinghoffer

All Rights Reserved

Published in the United States by Doubleday,
an imprint of The Doubleday Publishing Group,
a division of Random House, Inc., New York.
www.doubleday.com

DOUBLEDAY is a registered trademark and the DD colophon
is a trademark of Random House, Inc.

Book design by Kathryn Parise

Library of Congress Cataloging-in-Publication Data
Klinghoffer, David, 1965–
How would God vote? : why the Bible commands you to be a
conservative / David Klinghoffer. — 1st ed.
p. cm.
1. Religion and politics—United States. 2. Conservatism—United States. I. Title.
BL2525.K59 2008
261.7—dc22
2007043744

ISBN 978-0-385-51542-9

PRINTED IN THE UNITED STATES OF AMERICA

1 3 5 7 9 10 8 6 4 2

First Edition

For Jacob and Saul

CONTENTS

III. WORLD

HOW
WOULD
GOD VOTE?

✧

With God, or Against Him

✧

To anyone who takes God seriously, every election poses a radical question. Will we vote with Him, or against Him? The Bible is an unapologetically political book and an extremely conservative one. Some political views offend God, and those views are mostly liberal. To misperceive Scripture's political meaning is as much an error as to misperceive its moral meaning.

Yet liberal leaders and left-wing activists have obscured these clear truths. One thinks of Senator Hillary Clinton, who in a June 2007 forum on CNN claimed that it was her Christian beliefs that underlie her stands on controversial issues. With reference to herself and her fellow Democratic candidates, Clinton forthrightly said, "I think you can sense how we are attempting to try to inject faith into policy." That line alone, spoken by a Republican, would have been trumpeted on the front page of countless newspapers and Web sites as proof that the speaker harbors a secret plot to turn America into a theocracy along the lines of Iran or Saudi Arabia. Even a forthrightly Christian candidate like Mike Huckabee feels he has to be more cautious with his rhetoric than any Democrat does.

Most Republican politicians, in their usual timid fashion, would probably endorse the sentiment expressed by Religious Left guru Rev. Jim Wallis: "God is not a Republican or a Democrat." That sentiment is, however, obviously disingenuous. In his best-selling book *God's Politics,* Wallis makes it plain that he thinks Jesus was a left-liberal. Since the book came out in 2004, Wallis and his message have been taken up by the 2008 Democratic presidential contenders, who disguise in religious finery positions that in fact derive from a secular worldview, the very opposite of the biblical one.

As an Orthodox Jew, I offer this book as a call to arms to America's mostly Christian conservative voters. Some of those voters may follow other Republicans in feeling intimidated by Democratic rhetoric. They might be attracted to the advice of Evangelical former Bush aide David Kuo, who in his own best-selling memoir, *Tempting Faith,* advocates a "fast" from politics, a temporary break or abstention from practical advocacy: "By so passionately pursuing politics Christians have alienated their 'opponents' by giving the sense that to be Christian means to embrace certain policies. But the reality, of course, is that Christians can disagree about virtually any policy matter."

No, that's not the reality. Jews and Christians are free to think anything they want, however ridiculous. An American who says he bases his outlook on the Bible may turn out to believe in the tooth fairy as well, but that doesn't mean such belief finds support in Scripture. In fact, the Bible is as clear on politics as it is on morals. Plenty of Christians and Jews fail morally—I certainly do—but we would be wrong to pretend that, in doing so, we are being true to our religious beliefs. John McCain was right when he said, in a 2000 interview on beliefnet.com, that our "nation was founded primarily on Christian principles." That fact should have practical consequences.

It has become both more important than ever to state this openly and fearlessly. For we live in an era when faith is under sustained intellectual assault, and any suggestion of biblical religion's true political relevance is greeted with accusations of "theocracy."

A succession of New Atheist tracts shooting to the top of the best-seller list lately have seemed like distress flares launched from the deck of a foundering ship at sea. What happened to all that talk, once a favorite among conservatives, about America as a Christian nation? Surely the wildly enthusiastic reception bestowed on Christopher Hitchens's *God Is Not Great* and Richard Dawkins's *The God Delusion* signals that something has gone wrong with our supposedly religious national culture.

Yet even as the rise of the New Atheism signaled that the country's religious identity was less secure than previously thought, atheists and other advocates of secularism made a startling charge: that conservative religionists seek to foist theocracy on us all. As Dawkins himself observed, "Absolutism is far from dead. Indeed, it rules the minds of a great number of people in the world today, most dangerously so in the Muslim world and in the incipient American theocracy."

The charge has been echoed countless times from the political Left. Iran's rulers are classic theocrats, whose regime subjects their country to religious sharia law. Can we say the same of a Christian like George W. Bush? Indeed so, according to prominent recent books, including Kevin Phillip's *American Theocracy,* Rabbi James Rudin's *The Baptizing of America,* Michelle Goldberg's *Kingdom Coming: The Rise of Christian Nationalism,* and Chris Hedges's *American Fascists: The Christian Right and the War on America.* As Howard Dean, the Democratic National Committee chairman, asked after Bush sought to keep the brain-damaged Terri Schiavo from being dehydrated to death, "Are we going to live in a theocracy

where the highest powers tells us what to do?" Even a GOP legisla-
tor, Connecticut's Christopher Shays, has lamented that his party is
morphing into the "party of theocracy."

Is it true, as the atheists contend, that theocracy is implicit in the
idea of religious conservatism? Every conservative I know denies
this. A Christian leader I particularly admire, Charles Colson, calls
the theocracy accusation "a false and malicious charge, and our critics know it." I believe they do know it.

In fact, the secular think tank where I'm a senior fellow, the Discovery Institute, has been tarred with the charge of theocracy because of its advocacy of allowing high school teachers to introduce
mainstream scientific criticisms of Darwinian evolution in the classroom. In the discourse of the secularist Left, the word "theocracy"
functions as a synonym for "Silence them!"

But I hereby cast aside the fear of such slanders. Precisely because
our country is steadily losing its religious mooring, it is time to be
frank about what we want, or what we should want. No, it's not
the theocracy of secularist imagining. That is a canard, sheer propaganda. Instead, it is a democratic and constitutional government
but of a special kind: open to looking to the Bible for political wisdom. It is a biblically correct democracy.

My hope is to help Americans, especially those on the Right, stop
feeling so shy about God talk when we discuss what's best for our
country, to give people courage about applying biblical wisdom,
openly, in our public lives. This makes most conservatives nervous,
as if someone's going to accuse them of being a would-be mullah.
The conservative establishment's allergy to religious talk explains
the mass sneezing fit that greeted the sudden rise of Mike Huckabee,
a former Baptist pastor, as a serious presidential contender. But just
for a change, let's take the offensive and fight to alter the terms of
the debate, because we are not exactly winning the argument right
now. Pretending to fight "theocracy," secularists are in fact attempting a radical redirection of American life that seeks to silence the au-

thentic Judeo-Christian heritage that has sustained America since the country's inception.

Meanwhile the folks you'd expect to be defending tradition are strangely mute, unintentionally lending support to the outdated secular insistence that the Bible be kept out of politics. On issue after issue—abortion and gay marriage come readily to mind— "respectable" conservatives and Republicans feel obliged to make their case entirely without reference to the true biblical underpinnings of their beliefs. Everyone knows that scriptural teaching is the main reason most conservatives feel as they do about the leading moral-political questions, but we obey a virtual code of silence— *omerta,* as the Mafia would put it—about this fact. We sound defensive, weak, ashamed, and dishonest. Then we wonder why the field of 2008 Republican presidential contenders was perceived as so unexciting. We sincerely ponder the enigma of evaporating Evangelical Christian support for "conservatism." The proportion of Evangelicals who think of themselves as Republicans has sunk from 50 percent to 44 percent since 2004, reports John C. Green, a political scientist with the Pew Forum on Religion and Public Life.

Finally, finally, *please*—let's be brave and honest in stating what a biblical politics necessarily entails. That is what I do in this book, which examines twenty hot-button political issues in light of the scriptural worldview. What does God think about immigration? About gun control? About global warming? About the threat of so-called Islamofascism? It should go without saying that my political reading of the Bible is my own, drawing on the oldest biblical interpretive tradition, claiming roots that go back three thousand years and found in the Talmud and other ancient rabbinic texts. Yet Scripture's vision of the ideal society does not belong to Jews alone. A true Jewish and a true Christian politics are, I will argue, almost identical.

Such a vision is very different from that of secularism—including one way that will probably surprise and outrage many of my fellow conservatives. I refer to Chapter 20 of this book, which I introduce by noting how the Bible casts doubt on the neoconservative preoccupation with fighting "World War IV" against "Islamofascism." The Bible has a political vision and it is not neoconservative. It emphasizes the struggle against domestic cultural decay over a fight against foreign enemies.

Up till now, it has been impossible to have this conversation because conservatives were stampeded by political opponents. Now, despite the evidence of the New Atheist phenomenon that "Christian America" is weaker than ever, let us put our cards on the table— or if you prefer, on the altar. Everyone, I think, will be relieved, not only by the very act of giving ourselves permission to be frank, but also by what we'll find at the end of an honest inquiry into the politics of the Bible.

Yet this will all seem unthinkable to anyone who associates biblical politics with Iran or Saudi Arabia. The chief objection I will have to deal with before going on, then, is the question of whether the Bible can sit comfortably alongside the Constitution.

2

Theocracy on Main Street?

The Bible commands a style of politics that in the American context could only be described as deeply conservative. Is, then, the politics of God theocratic?

A strong case could be made for theocracy, American-style, if the word were defined not in the conventional way but according to its root meaning. Democracy signifies the rule of the *demos,* the people. Strictly speaking, theocracy means the rule not of churches or priests but of *theos,* God. It won't do to deny that many conservatives, even while unambiguously affirming the traditional American separation of church and state, would add more *theos* to the democratic mix than is currently the case. I choose not to call myself a theocrat because I know how eager liberal secularists would be to twist the word against me. Dishonestly they would make it appear that I wish to impose a literal biblical theocracy, that I would dumbly imitate word for word the political structure of king, priesthood, and religious high court that existed in biblical antiquity.

Yet, in a subtler sense, are we not all theocrats now? So you might have thought when, in 2006, Barack Obama declared, "Secularists are wrong when they ask believers to leave their religion at the door before entering into the public square." Certainly, the etiquette of the current presidential campaign has allowed Democrats free rein to invoke the Almighty, even as it denies that right to Republicans. "We have chosen to keep our politics unilluminated by divine revelation," intones Columbia University professor Mark Lilla in his recent book, *The Stillborn God: Religion, Politics, and the Modern West* (2007). Hardly! Approaching the 2008 election, the Democratic candidates were "carefully marinated in Scripture," as *Time* magazine put it, a far cry from Howard Dean's religion-allergic presidential campaign four years earlier. Dean bluntly said, "My religion doesn't inform my public policy." Though Dean is today chairman of the Democratic National Committee, his secularist war cry has been thoroughly abandoned—by Democrats. In proposing immigration reform, Hillary Clinton quotes the New Testament for support. Today, there are many on the Left who would claim to be inspired by the question, What would Jesus do? Al Gore, for one. In their heart, religious conservatives might ask themselves the same question, but most are too fearful to face up openly to the full implications of a biblical politics or to express those implications in public. This book speaks to the shy and hesitant, urging them to take courage, in the manner of the biblical prophets. It's time to bring the Bible unapologetically into the maelstrom of American politics.

If the Bible is all that it's cracked up to be by the faithful, however, namely a reflection of God's own mind expressed in human language, then why would only a few religious weirdos contemplate enacting its legislation as it appears in the scriptural text? For one thing, the Bible almost never means what it seems to mean when read in literal fashion as if you were reading a newspaper. However, if we did try to read the Bible that way, we would right away smack up against the fact that the Bible *literally* addresses itself to a Jewish commonwealth where most of the citizens are farmers. America is neither a Jewish country nor a predominantly agricultural society. On those grounds alone, a simpleminded political reading of the Bible has to be rejected.

More to the point, America is a constitutional republic, and that is not going to change. No one wants it to change. America is also a pluralist society that, even though the Founders certainly envisioned a Christian country, today contentedly tolerates many religions and enforces none. No one wants that to change either. Any religiously inspired daydream to the contrary would result in political policy prescriptions that are strictly dead on arrival.

Instead, what I have in mind is to draw out the larger principles of the Bible's political vision. On the question of what those principles are, there has been much disagreement. Biblical politics is not exclusively a right-wing preoccupation. Both abolition and civil rights were essentially religious crusades. And in the nineteenth and twentieth centuries, socialism was, for many (like Leo Tolstoy), explicitly derived from the egalitarian teachings of Jesus. In this country, the Social Gospel movement was frankly touted as a form of Christian socialism. So don't believe it when you hear that only the Right seeks to enshrine its religious values in practical law.

Nor is it only liberal Christians such as Gore and Mrs. Clinton who would do so. The most aggressive and intolerant theocrats are ideologues like Richard Dawkins. But isn't he an atheist? Sure, but Mitt Romney got it exactly right when he said, in 2007, that secularists seem "intent on establishing a new religion in America—the religion of secularism." For each element in the Judeo-Christian family of faiths, aggressive secularism has its counterpart: a strict ethical code, focusing on health issues ("Thou shalt not smoke," etc.); the use of shame when individuals disregard ethical rules (e.g., fat people); a related promise of eternal life through medical advances; a creation story (Darwinian evolution); a threatened apocalypse heralding the end of civilization (catastrophic climate change); and so forth. All that's missing is a deity, but not every religion has one, as the case of Zen Buddhism attests. The Secular Church is populous and dynamic, with a membership far exceeding the figure of 7.5 percent of Americans who identify themselves as "secular." Many individuals who identify nominally as Jews or Christians in fact are devout secularists.

Secularism would write into law many of its religious beliefs, with punishments for those who fail to comply. Draconian anti-smoking laws, legislation against the use of trans fats in restaurants, and calls to radically restrict fossil fuel use even at the cost of crippling the world's economy are a few examples. In the upside-down "moralesque" (as I've called it) behavioral code of secularism, avoiding physical illness is held to be the heaviest moral, not merely pragmatic, obligation. Thus, in the presidential race in 2007, John Edwards opined that under his proposed scheme of socialized medicine, not only would every American be required to be covered but everyone would also be required to visit a doctor for regular check-ups. The plan "requires that everybody get preventive care," he explained. "You have to go in and be checked and make sure that you are OK." That might be fine if the choice of seeking care were left up to individual Americans. When the right "choice" is imposed on us, what is that but coercive secular theocracy?

Young children are plainly being targeted for conversion to secularism, including in public schools. Thus the angry resistance from secularists to any argument that a teacher might have the right, as a matter of academic freedom, to discuss scientific critiques of orthodox Darwinism in biology class. Meanwhile, the Anti-Defamation League—a group that is Jewish only in the sense that bagels are Jewish—has been advocating a reading list of "anti-bias" books for children of kindergarten age through sixth grade. Two of the recommended books are *Gloria Goes to Gay Pride* ("A young girl participates in the Gay Pride Day parade," as the ADL's Web site summarizes the book) and *My Two Uncles* ("A young child's grandfather has trouble accepting the fact that his son is gay"). Any child who takes to heart the message of these books would be adopting, among other things, a bias in favor of the secular teaching that endorses homosexuality.

What's so insidious about secular theocracy is that it's enacted under the false pretense of being mere common sense, or ironclad science, beyond debate. At least Christian and Jewish liberals are more honest, plainly admitting that they seek a religious basis for their favorite laws. They have every right to make their pitch for the Bible as the urtext of social progressivism.

However, conservatives make a far more compelling claim on Scripture as a support for their views. I have known many people, Jews and Christians, who as they grew up or grew older became more religious than they had been earlier in life. Of that group of born-again or repentant believers, I know of some whose political views were unaffected by spiritual growth. I know many more, in fact most in this unscientific sampling, who became more politically conservative as they became more religious. I have never met one, not one individual, who as a result of becoming more engaged with the Bible became more politically liberal. There may be one somewhere. There may also be a Bigfoot.

What are the chances, however, that, even taking the Bible in this more philosophical way, we'll arrive at a result like that in koranic theocracy? Happily, the chances are nil. That becomes evident if you first consider the biblical roots of the idea of government by God, then how scriptural teaching was translated into practice in Europe and America, and finally what binds together the set of policy prescriptions identified in the pages to follow with a biblical worldview.

⟡

Scripture makes an unlikely basis for an absolutist, Iranian-style theocracy, but a congenial one for a constitutional government of the kind envisioned by the Founders. The Bible on the desk of frequently vilified Christian leaders and alleged theocrats like Charles Colson or James Dobson has two parts, the New and the Old Testaments. The New Testament is remarkably nonpolitical, making a sharp differentiation between God's kingdom and the kingdom of man. As Jesus put it, "My kingship is not of this world" (John 18:36). He also said, "Render therefore to Caesar the things that are Caesar's, and to God the things that are God's" (Matthew 22:21). Teachings like these don't lend themselves very easily to any political interpretation—which is unsurprising since the early Church, at any rate, understood Jesus and Paul to have taught that the world would end soon, within the lifetime of some of those who heard them preach. It would have made little sense to begin sketching the outlines of a church-run government. The clear distinction between God's affairs and man's was carried on by Christian theology, as in Augustine's *City of God,* which he contrasted with the City of Man. In the Middle Ages, the official philosopher of the Catholic Church, Thomas Aquinas, perceived a similar distinction between religious and secular authority.

But what of the Jewish Bible, the Old Testament, which anyone who takes Scripture seriously can't ignore?

A glance through the Hebrew Scriptures could leave the impression that taking Moses and his teaching to heart means establishing a regime based exclusively on religious law. The Torah—also known as the Pentateuch or Five Books of Moses, the first books in the Bible and in many ways the very heart of Scripture—envisions religious courts imposing capital punishment for offenses like Sabbath desecration and homosexual intercourse. Sounds pretty terrifying. Few of us would wish to live in the handful of Christian states in relatively modern times that have made brief experiments of literally implementing Old Testament legislation—by, for example, executing adulterous wives. The Reformed Protestant societies (Calvin's Geneva in the sixteenth century, Puritan England under Cromwell in the seventeenth) made significant if brief headway in trying to translate Hebrew law into practice. Their experiments were reckoned notorious failures. The Pilgrims who settled in Massachusetts in 1620 also took the Old Testament legal framework literally as a model, but this attempt lasted only a generation or two and was abandoned.

However, the Hebrew Bible itself pictures its laws as those of an operating government only in two circumstances: the ancient Israelite past and the Messianic future. The latter assumes the rule of a promised Messiah, for which Jews and Christians have been waiting, with their different understandings of the concept, for thousands of years. That time isn't here. In the Messianic future, according to the Hebrew prophets, human nature will be radically transformed. It thus seems unlikely that there will be a need to execute Sabbath breakers or homosexuals. Even if, hypothetically, there were such a need in the promised Messianic world, the penal code enshrined in the Bible is structured so as to be remarkably resistant to actually imposing religiously mandated penalties on most classes of criminals. In a criminal trial, the standards for admitting testimony of eyewitnesses were highly exacting. More important, to receive punishment upon his body (death or scourging), a wrongdoer prior to the act had to be warned by two witnesses that what he was about to do carried such a penalty. This warning had to be given *immediately* prior to the act. What's more, the criminal, in response to the witnesses' warning, must give a clear verbal affirmation that he understands the warning and that he *willingly accepts the punishment*. If these amazing conditions were met, and if he went ahead and committed the act anyway, and if acceptable witnesses testified to it all before the court—then he could receive lashes or one of four different sorts of death penalties (stoning, beheading, strangling, or burning).

According to rabbinic tradition, certain crimes described in the Torah were never even once *committed and punished* in the history of the Jewish people from the giving of the Torah at Mount Sinai, through the kingdom of David, on until the first century of the common era, a period of some thirteen hundred years. After that, the Jews were exiled from their land and never again even theoretically had the power of inflicting an execution. So in the earlier period, of Jewish sovereignty, were the people continually in chaos with criminals acting freely without fear of punishment? Or was everybody a saint or an angel? No. Instead, according to Jewish law, the king of the nation was empowered to impose criminal penalties for the sake of keeping the society at peace.

Did the king then represent theocratic rule? Not really. He was a governmental figure who may not easily be categorized as either religious or secular. On one hand, the Torah required that he set an example of piety. He must, for example, carry a Torah scroll with him at all times. On the other hand, justice meted out by the monarch was not governed by the laws that guided the religious courts. His justice was determined by prudence, not by divine decrees. He also could be appointed to his position by either a religious procedure or a secular one. Some kings of the Jewish state were chosen by prophets who spoke for God. Others were chosen democratically, by popular acclaim. It was, on the whole, an interesting mix of secular and religious government, with the emphasis in practice falling more on the secular than on the religious. Certainly it was a more "religious" government even than any conservative Republican today advocates as a model for twenty-first-century America. But the mix of sacred and secular was not wildly different from the traditional American mix. The religious laws that sound so foreign were more a theoretical construct of what justice meant in God's mind, to be studied for moral and spiritual edification, than they were a practical basis of government. Those laws emerge from principles that are at the foundation of American civilization.

Our country in its politics from early on was influenced by the Bible, laying stress on a general framework of morality drawn from Scripture. It is helpful to listen to the words of people who were there and saw with their own eyes the relationship of politics to religion in the new republic. The French aristocrat Alexis de Tocqueville, who traveled about the land in 1831 and reported on his findings with an emphasis on political institutions, extols the religiosity of Americans: "There is no country in the world where the Christian religion retains a greater influence over the souls of men than in America." He says elsewhere, "On my arrival in the United States the religious aspect of the country was the first thing that struck my attention; and the longer I stayed there, the more I perceived the great political consequences resulting from this new state of things."

Tocqueville wrote of how dependent the maintenance of liberty was on a widespread faith in God. Without religion and religion-based morality, it has to be the government that restrains men from expending their energy and their country's resources on vice. Tasking government with that job is, of course, a sure recipe for tyranny. So America required a strong religious tradition. But for that tradition to remain strong, it had to be separate from the government.

Tocqueville didn't mean to say that religion should be totally divorced from public life—but rather only from directly managing the machinery of the state. His idea of the "separation of church and state," as he observed it personally in the early American republic, would today send the secularist lawyers from the ACLU scrambling to the barricades, blowing trumpets, and shouting at the top of their lungs that a fascist theocracy was upon us. "Religion in America," he wrote, "takes no direct part in the government of society, but it must be regarded as the first of their political institutions; for if it does not impart a taste for freedom, it facilitates the use of it."

Tocqueville tells of a story he read in a New York state newspaper about a judge who dismissed a witness in a court case because the man declared himself an atheist. According to the news summary, the judge commented that "he had not before been aware that there was a man living who did not believe in the existence of God; that this belief constituted the sanction of all testimony in a court of justice; and that he knew of no cause in a Christian country where a witness had been permitted to testify without such a belief." The newspaper, as Tocqueville pointed out, found this judicial decision unremarkable and passed over it as if what the judge had expressed was a sentiment shared by all, which evidently it was. The curious point that lay behind the article, from the reporter's perspective, was not that the man's testimony was rejected but that anyone would publicly affirm his disbelief in the Deity and expect to be admitted to testify in court.

In the century and a quarter or so that followed, the general tone of public life was deeply respectful of traditional faith. Historian and JFK biographer Thomas C. Reeves (*A Question of Character: A Life of John F. Kennedy*) gives a snapshot of our nation's overwhelmingly Christian culture under the Truman, Eisenhower, and Kennedy administrations: "In this 'golden age of American churches,' Bishop Fulton J. Sheen and evangelist Billy Graham used their considerable oratorical and intellectual talents on radio and television to inspire millions. Newspapers carried regular columns by both clergymen and published a great deal of religious news. Highly popular magazines like *Time* and the *Reader's Digest* contained numerous stories filled with Christian messages. . . . Hollywood gave us *A Man Called Peter*, a highly favorable biography of a Protestant clergyman. Businesses routinely closed on Sunday. . . . Few quibbled about identifying America as a Christian nation. It was and had always been." How did we get from there to here?

Today we are in the middle of a culture war, pitting secularists against religionists. One prize in this war is the reins of government. Christian conservatives were not the initial aggressors in this struggle. An article in the journal *The Public Interest* by two political scientists, Louis Bolce and Gerald de Maio, reminds us of the prehistory of the culture war. The authors trace American political culture from the 1960s, asserting that the 1972 Democratic National Convention marked a decisive turning point. That year, secularists took over the Democratic Party: "Prior to the late 1960s, there was something of a tacit commitment among elites in both parties to the traditional Judeo-Christian teachings regarding authority, sexual mores, and the family. This consensus was shattered in 1972 when the Democratic Party was captured by a faction whose cultural reform agenda was perceived by many (both inside and outside the convention) as antagonistic to traditional religious values."

Certainly, the Christian atmosphere that Tocqueville noted had dissipated by 1973, when the Supreme Court issued *Roe v. Wade,* making abortion a constitutional right. Within a few years, religious conservatives organized in response, finding refuge among the Republicans. The recent battle over gay marriage is just the latest effort by secular activists to transform our country.

It is only if we imagine that American history began in 1980, when the so-called Christian Right helped Ronald Reagan win the White House, that religious conservatives look like they are seizing political terrain they never occupied before. Just the opposite is true. They are only trying to restore the status quo that had prevailed before 1972, certainly before the 1960s, when everyone agreed that very general scriptural principles formed the basis of our way of life.

It is that kind of America whose restoration I call for here, the outline of whose policies, updated for today, I seek to describe in the coming pages. I shall divide the discussion into three parts. In the first part, I deal with political issues that affect mainly the private sphere, that of the family: marriage and the role of women, gay marriage and homosexuality, parenthood, abortion, and the education of young people. In the second, I move on to issues with a national or societal focus: poverty and homelessness, business and taxes, health care, drug legalization and smoking bans, capital punishment, racism and affirmative action, gun control, free speech, and privacy. Finally, I widen the focus to include issues relating to our country's interaction with the rest of the world: immigration, the environment, war, the Islamic threat, support for Israel, and the sinister shadow of Europe.

You may notice something right away about this list of political hot potatoes, which will suggest to us a further reason why biblical politics is compatible with political liberty, and with that I will conclude this introduction.

An overlooked enigma of political life is why there are distinct ideological groupings at all. Doesn't it seem equally if not more plausible to imagine a scenario where people's opinions on political issues formed no patterns at all? For example, there seems to be nothing that links Al Gore–style worrying about climate change with favoring state-sanctioned gay marriage. Yet somehow they go together. If you meet a partisan of abortion rights, it's a good bet that person will be favorably inclined toward banning smoking in public spaces. The converse also applies. Conservatives are equally predictable. Curious, isn't it? We take the liberal-conservative divide for granted, rarely pausing to contemplate how mysterious it actually is.

Well, the Hebrew Bible solves the mystery. The solution can be found in the unexpected context of the seemingly primitive and bizarre laws of ritual contamination, on which Scripture lavishes loving attention. The relevant material is laid out in dense detail mainly in the Bible's third book, Leviticus, aka the stuff most Jews skip over in synagogue as most Christians do in church. Let's spend a moment delving into this unfamiliar but highly relevant material.

When you are in a state of contamination, there are certain ritual activities, mainly having to do with the great Jerusalem Temple that was destroyed almost two thousand years ago, in which you would be forbidden to participate. In every case, a key to cleansing impurity is ritualized immersion in water, whether of the whole body or just the hands.

So-called ritual contamination and impurity are two common but very dysfunctional translations of the Hebrew *tumah*. The corresponding term *taharah* is translated, again unsatisfactorily, as "purity." According to the Bible, here is a list of things that will render you "contaminated" (*tameh*): touching a human corpse or the carcass of certain animals; having a seminal emission; menstruating; giving birth; suffering the effects of a supernaturally induced skin affliction, *tzaraat*—unknown to medicine today but vividly described by Scripture. It's all in Leviticus, with amplification across pages upon pages of the Talmud, which in turn adds other activities to the list. For example, sleeping contaminates the hands.

Remember, we are seeking the general philosophical principles that underlie such laws. My assumption, which should be the assumption of anyone who takes the Bible seriously, is that all of this strange and ancient text—including the parts thought to be tedious for modern readers—has something crucial to teach us about the proper ordering of a society's public and private life. Otherwise why did God give it to us? Or if you prefer a less religious perspective, why was it preserved and practiced down through so many generations? I find that the less familiar passages in Scripture, looked at closely and with sympathy, have no less instructive value than the parts we think we already know well.

Yet how could any of this remarkably obscure stuff about ritual contamination be relevant to twenty-first-century American politics? On the contrary, it sounds hopelessly arcane and backward, like something out of Frazer's *Golden Bough*. Don't be fooled.

Modern secular Bible scholars, those geniuses, have figured out that contamination has something to do with death. That leaves much unexplained. A fuller illumination of the matter can be found in the famous Torah commentary by Samson Raphael Hirsch (1808–1888), a German rabbi celebrated as the chief early representative of Modern Orthodoxy. In the course of this book, I will be introducing the perspectives of many classical interpreters of Scripture, mainly (but not exclusively) Jewish because that is the tradition I know best and that I find most compelling. Hirsch, among the more recent of those I'll be quoting, was a contemporary of Darwin, whose philosophical framework was that of materialism, the view that sees man's situation in the world as being entirely determined by material forces, not spiritual ones. Hirsch countered that the Bible, through the ritual contamination laws, seeks to inoculate us against exactly that spirit-denying, nature-exalting worldview that achieved dominance in the nineteenth century—and still afflicts us.

Here is how that comes out. Every source of *tumah*, contamination, bears a resemblance to death in that it conveys an illusory message that people are entrapped in nature, their consciousness determined by material forces, rather than their being free to make moral choices. A dead body has been robbed of any possibility of making free decisions. It has been defeated by nature. So a corpse is the source of the most severe contamination. Hirsch similarly explains all the contaminating experiences. In each—birth, menstruation, seminal emission, the weird disease of *tzaraat*, sleep—the person temporarily loses control of his body. Any of these conditions could leave the damaging, materialistic, and false impression that we are slaves to nature.

In the biblical view, by contrast, we are free to choose to follow God's commandments. We'd have to be, otherwise His commanding us to do right makes little sense. Rejecting materialism is thus essential to the moral life. Hirsch wrote, commenting on Leviticus 11:46–47: "All these [contamination laws] are truths which, in the face of human frailty and the powers of the forces of nature which the appearance of death preaches, are to be brought again and again to the minds of living people, so that they remain conscious of their unique position of freedom in the midst of the physical world, and remain forever armed in proud consciousness of their freedom, armed against the doctrine of materialism." The "cure" for *tumah* is immersion in water because this entails the free and conscious will to cleanse oneself. This is why, in Judaism, ritual hand-washing—for example, upon waking up in the morning or before eating bread—is accomplished by filling a cup with water and then pouring the water over your hands. Just putting your hands under a faucet would be too passive.

Here's where it gets uncomfortable for the Left. The understanding of liberalism as the political expression of materialism will be familiar to many political conservatives. I first heard the formulation from writer and radio commentator Michael Medved, who is also a friend and neighbor. But the Bible made the same connection millennia ago. Virtually every liberal position on a hot-button issue can be explained this way. Some lefty views emphasize, as Hirsch put it, the "powers of the forces of nature."

Gay marriage: The implicit justification for this insists that gays are in the grip of nature. They have no choice about their sexual behavior. So let's endorse their love in civil law.

Abortion: Here it's women who are supposedly in the grip of nature, specifically sexual desire. The lady made a mistake and got pregnant. Liberals believe she can't be held responsible for this, as denying her an abortion would do. The solution to unwanted pregnancy is a material one (ten minutes of vacuuming the uterus) over a spiritual one (taking responsibility for the outcome of sexual intercourse).

Global warming: We are in the grip of a vengeful, enraged nature! "Angry nature is holding a gun to our heads," as the magazine of the Sierra Club warns, among similar voices of environmentalist warning.

Other liberal views don't make an issue of nature as such but still implicitly deny what Hirsch calls our "unique position of freedom," advocating material mechanisms to keep us safe and happy rather than relying on free choice.

Health care: Rather than leave health decisions up to the individual, many liberals would like to impose government-directed "universal health care."

Health regulations: Laws banning smoking in public or the use of trans fats in restaurant cooking take responsibility for one's health out of the hands of the individual and give it over to the government. So long, "unique position of freedom."

Education: Conservative education philosophy, expressed in the preference for school choice or home-schooling, is all about giving freedom and responsibility to parents. Liberal philosophy transfers responsibility to the state, or to teachers' unions.

And so on. Liberal views, far from being random, actually form the political expression of a comprehensive worldview—in biblical terms, *tumah*-thinking. It was to counteract this perspective that the Bible proposed its system of ritual contamination and purification. God established the Jews as a people to make exactly the kinds of distinctions I have tried to highlight here. "For I, God, am He that brings you up out of the land of Egypt to be your God . . . to distinguish between the pure and the impure" (Leviticus 11:45–47).* I realize the irony in the fact that we Jews are today, sociologically speaking, in the forefront of those advocating a liberal or *tumah*-driven political value system.

---

* Biblical citations throughout are from Rabbi Nosson Scherman, ed., Stone Edition Tanach (Brooklyn, NY: Mesorah Publications, 1998).

Looked at this way, it becomes apparent why religious Americans gravitate to conservatism. By far the majority of them are Christians and their biblical religion is premised on the idea of individual moral responsibility. Generally speaking, liberalism distrusts the individual, whereas conservatism trusts him enough to give him a chance to make the right, or the wrong, decision. If he makes the wrong one, he will have to answer to his own conscience, or to his God. That is, assuming that making the wrong choice will not adversely affect other people and their freedom to make the right choice. That helps us understand, as we shall see, why a scripturally informed conservatism is not libertarian on certain issues where other people are negatively impacted (for example, abortion) or where the whole tone of society is adversely affected (for example, illicit drug use).

In general, though, religious faith presumes that God commands us to act in certain ways—which in turn presumes moral responsibility and the freedom to exercise it. This is an excellent reason why a biblical politics, while seeking to bring a religious perspective to bear on the formulation of policies, would never be theocratic in the nightmare totalitarian style of Iran or Saudi Arabia. Scripture implicitly prescribes a system of ordered liberty. Of just what kind, how specifically it would be articulated in the twenty political issues addressed in this book, we'll see shortly.

Not all Democrats, of course, fully accept the strictly "liberal" or *tumah* view, but they belong to a party that, of the two main parties in American political life, is the one identified with the belief that moral choices are profoundly conditioned by circumstances and therefore aren't truly free. Which is why, looking to the future, it is of interest that the Bible carries on with the theme of cleansing *tumah*. In the words of Ezekiel, a prophet who foresaw the End of Days, quoting God: "Son of Man, the House of Israel dwell on their land, and they have contaminated it with their way and with their acts." In the end, however, "I will sprinkle pure water upon you, that you may become cleansed; I will cleanse you from all your contamination and from all your idols" (36:17, 25).

Liberals will be in particular need of that shower.

It may, in short, be too much to suggest that God himself is a Republican. In fact, a truly Bible-centered politics will put believers at odds with both parties. Far less so with the GOP, however, but certainly at some points. If the Bible is to be allowed the full range of its deserved influence over the democratic process, one question that's bound to arise is how the religious American should evaluate individual candidates who may get some of their views "right" as the Bible would define them, while getting others wrong. Should you vote for the man or woman who gets seventeen right over the candidate who gets only fifteen? Is there a litmus test issue? I would argue that there are a couple. But we'll come to that soon.

I

$\diamondsuit$

FAMILY

$\diamondsuit$

3

Women's Issues:
All in the Family

With half the population having a direct stake in the matter, the commonest worry about a biblically correct democracy is how women would fare. The erstwhile Republican analyst Kevin Phillips, for example, wrote a best-selling book called *American Theocracy* (2006), noting the "perception that some religious conservatives have a somewhat Taliban-like philosophy—or perhaps simply an Old Testament one—of returning women to their traditional place in a world of male supremacy." We are meant to conjure up a picture of America's females all zipped up in burkas and following meekly behind their husbands as the muezzin over the shopping mall loudspeaker declaims verses from the book of Deuteronomy.

In truth, the place of women in an authentically scriptural government would be all about protecting freedom in the long term, a far cry from Taliban-style oppression. Recall what we just said about biblical statecraft and its focus on always recalling to our minds our moral responsibility. That entails the liberty to exercise your free will. Compelled wearing of burkas will not be on our menu.

The idea that biblical politics means true liberation for women will come as a surprise to some liberal Democrats. In 2008, America witnessed the first full-scale presidential campaign by a woman. Senator Hillary Clinton's self-projected image as the "Champion of Women," as her own Web site calls her, comprises a series of policy preferences that sound superficially like the very quintessence of the will to give women their liberty.

Mrs. Clinton listed her positions on a series of issues. She objects to the fact that working women earn only 77 cents for every dollar earned by a man. She supports equal pay laws such as the Paycheck Fairness Act. She favors a woman's "right to choose" (that curious euphemism). She would increase access to "family planning services" (more abortion, plus contraceptives). She would require health insurance companies to cover contraception, with measures like the Prevention First Act. She takes credit for forcing the FDA to approve the Plan B "morning after" pill, yet another contraceptive. Not least, she would "expand access to affordable, high-quality childcare" (subsidized or run by the government).

Something that unites all liberal policy positions relating to women is that they seek to ease the way to separating women from child-rearing. This is a back door to undermining freedom, not strengthening it. To see why, we need to back up some thousands of years to the Bible's narrative of the creation of the first man and woman. We'll then leapfrog forward in scriptural history to the story of the Egyptian enslavement, where some of Adam and Eve's descendants, the Jews, faced a radical challenge to marriage. Liberals like Kevin Phillips associate the Bible with a moral framework in opposition to equality between the sexes. The truth is more interesting.

⟡

When God set Adam and Eve in the Garden of Eden, it was initially a paradise of egalitarianism. Arguably, it was even a gynecocracy, a society where woman rules. The first couple were seduced by a "Serpent" (which I put in quotation marks because it wasn't a talking snake but a subtle spiritual force). Their act of rebellion against God, urged upon them by this serpent, was to eat the fruit of a forbidden tree. The Serpent knew who was in charge, for he "was cunning beyond any beast of the field" (Genesis 3:1). So he went with his subversive proposal, not to Adam, but to Eve. Would this make any sense in a world dominated by men?

As the man later told God, "The woman whom You gave to be with me—she gave me of the tree, and I ate" (3:12). It was a reasonable defense, for Adam knew that God would be aware how the power dynamic with Eve functioned.

Before the great sin of disobedience, Adam and Eve lived in an entirely domestic world. In the Garden of Eden, all their needs that we would associate with seeking the fruit of labor outside the home were taken care of. In this home environment, Eve was naturally dominant. The work of Eden was meant to be raising children who would raise children of their own after them. This was the only positive directive given to humans while they were still in Paradise: "God blessed them and God said to them, 'Be fruitful and multiply, fill the earth and subdue it' " (1:28).

In this scenario, Eve was the primary actor, with Adam relegated to a distant secondary role. It has always been this way with women and men, at least in the home, as George Gilder observes in his wise book *Men and Marriage* (1986). Unlike women, men continually have to prove themselves as men because their nature-dictated role in fruitful multiplying is so minimal. Without a free-willed moral act, man's contribution may be finished in a few minutes. Erection, ejaculation, all over. By the nature of his anatomy, a man is all but dispensable, almost pathetic. The Bible speaks of a man's need to "leave his father and his mother and cling to his wife" (2:24). What could be more pitiful than this childlike "clinging"?

Not so with the independently significant woman, critically important to the child's life. Her anatomy necessitates that she spend at least nine months nurturing her offspring. After it is born, she is provided with the necessities of feeding the child for years. Without her merciful agreement to have her husband in the home, he has no place there.

Only after the sin did man and woman leave the Garden for a different reality, the world of work. The changed conditions of existence meant that life's necessities would be much harder to secure now. This was to be the case both with the work of child-rearing—"in pain shall you bear children," God tells Eve—and the man's new and unaccustomed work of pursuing a career—"By the sweat of your brow shall you eat bread," God tells Adam (3:16, 3:19).

Finally, the male of the species had come into his own. Now he had a job to do that the woman could not if she was to perform her own task well, busy as she was bearing children in pain—both physical and spiritual, since children are not trained pets but free-willed and rebellious creatures themselves. At last, male and female are equal in their separate realms of endeavor. She will now be a "help opposite unto him" (2:18), as God intended her to be from the beginning. Man and woman have opposite, separate roles—he going out into the world to work, compensating for the loss of Eden, she remaining in the home, reproducing Eden behind the doors of the family home. As Rabbi Hirsch, whom we met in the previous chapter, notes in his commentary on the verses, this "certainly expresses no idea of subordination, but rather complete equality."

True, God says to Eve about this new relationship with Adam, "He shall rule over you" (3:16). However, he rules only in his own sphere, while she will always do so in hers. As George Gilder observes: "It is female power, organic and constitutional, that is real—holding sway over the deepest levels of consciousness, sources of happiness, and processes of social survival. Male dominance in the marketplace . . . might be considered more the ideological myth. It is designed to induce the majority of men to accept a bondage to the machine and the marketplace, to a large extent in the service of women."

Why does all this matter? Because Scripture perceives the family as the basis of a society where free will decisions can be made. Indeed, while I indicated earlier that the classical scriptural model of governance was threefold—king, courts, priesthood—in truth another and more basic structure underlies them all: the *bet av,* the parental house.

Power means the freedom to make decisions. Decisions can be made by individuals or by groups. The bigger the group making the decision, the closer we get to the idea of government, making choices on behalf of the people it claims to represent, who devolve their responsibility onto it. The more powerful the government, the more all-encompassing its role, the less responsibility any individual has. The smaller the group making the decision, the more it looks like a family, and the more moral responsibility each individual has. When the family is dispersed from the home, when the home is not a place where the wife nurtures children and creates an environment of refreshment and inspiration, when the home is merely the location of the beds in which the members of the "family" sleep at night, then any chance of the family exercising its power to make choices has been radically undermined. There is no family anymore. Just the house and the beds.

In the liberal political vision, that is a congenial outcome. After all, a fundamental assumption of liberalism holds that the bigger the group making the decisions, the better those decision are likely to be. So the focus of power ought to be the federal government, or better yet the United Nations.

The scriptural vision holds the opposite. Individuals engaged in "free-willed moral acts" (in Rabbi Hirsch's phrase) is the Bible's picture of an ideal society. Naturally there is a need for governance, but the closer we get to relying on the family for this, instead of on larger entities, the greater the likelihood of people taking their individual moral responsibilities to heart.

No one understood this better than Pharaoh, king of Egypt.

We turn to the narrative of the enslavement of the Jews, told in the book of Exodus. Twenty generations separated Adam and Eve from their descendant Abraham, considered the first Jew. Abraham's grandson Jacob, also called Israel, had twelve sons, who became the progenitors of the twelve tribes of Israel. The family went down to Egypt from the land of Canaan, initially to survive a famine. But they stayed and multiplied, finally being reduced there to slavery.

Pharaoh and his people feared the power of these Israelites, with their family-based social system. The Egyptian slave owners sought a way to break the power of their potentially rebellious servants. And in the worldview of biblical tradition, to accomplish this, it was only natural that Egypt would strike at the Jewish power base, the family.

Part of this strategy is indicated explicitly in the text, part as a matter of ancient oral tradition. The Egyptians imposed aggressive family planning. Since there was no Plan B pill then, Pharaoh opted for a cruder course, ordering the country's midwives to murder any newborn Hebrew boy: "When you deliver the Hebrew women, and you see them on the birthstool; if it is a son, you are to kill him, and if it is a daughter, she shall live" (Exodus 1:16). It really didn't matter whether he liquidated the boys or the girls. Either way, the next generation of Jewish families would be decimated.

Equally devastating was the Egyptian plot against Hebrew adults. Every year at Passover, Jews from time immemorial have sat down at their seder meal to recite the text of the Haggada. It is a meditation on the meaning of the Exodus from Egypt and includes some very old *midrashim* (rabbinic interpolations) on the biblical text. Considered to have been passed down orally from even more deeply antique times, a *midrash* (singular) is a tradition that fills in details that are unspecified, or unclearly specified, in the plain, often cryptic scriptural text.

The Haggada quotes a biblical verse, recalling the situation of the Jews in Egypt: "We cried to the Lord, the God of our fathers, and the Lord heard our voice. He saw our ill-treatment, our burden and our oppression" (Deuteronomy 26:7). Why the seeming redundancy? The Bible doesn't waste words, so each of those three expressions of pain ("ill-treatment," "burden," "oppression") must mean something different from the other two. Of the "oppression" endured by the Hebrews, the Haggada explains, "This refers to the breakup of their family life." But what does that mean? Another rabbinic text, *Midrash Tanchuma* (Buber ed.), dating back at least to the fifth century C.E., transmits the tradition that the Egyptian oppressors reversed the responsibilities of men and women. Rather than men slaving away "with mortar and with bricks, and with every labor of the field" (Exodus 1:14), it was women who performed this work. Meanwhile, men were cast into domestic roles, caring for families and homes.

The way to "break up family life," to overturn the power base comprised by the parental home, is through contraception, abortion, and sending women out to work in the fields—or in their "field," as we would say. Pharaoh was quite the Champion of Women.

We are left with what seems a paradox but really isn't. Secular liberalism insists it only wants to "free" women—and men too. Besides providing birth control and encouraging women to leave their children with caretakers and join the workforce, it would deregulate marriage altogether. That sounds like a trumpet call for liberty. Indeed, the deregulation of marriage is almost complete. A turning point was in 1969 when California became the first state to allow "no fault" divorce, meaning that either spouse could terminate a marriage at will without having to produce evidence of immoral or abusive acts by the other spouse. By the mid-1980s, every other state in the union had followed suit. The discourse of liberalism on marriage is replete with words like "autonomy," "self-fulfillment," and "choice." Implicitly, it teaches that society has no stake in the institution of marriage. Partners should be free to come and go from the relationship as they please.

The Bible, again, begs to differ. Marriage is institutionalized sexuality. Sexuality is very much a public concern. This is why the biblical commandment of circumcising infant boys (Leviticus 12:3) is carried out, by tradition, in daylight and in public, with a communal audience.

I anticipate the objection that the Bible *appears* to be on the side of constraining liberty. Would it, to take a very political question, countenance a woman's liberty to run for president? One needs to be honest. "You shall set over yourself a king," according to the book of Deuteronomy (17:15), not a queen. So biblical tradition understands that verse. Nor may a woman fill any public office. See the classical medieval sage Maimonides's authoritative legal code, the *Mishneh Torah* (Laws of Kings and Their Wars 1:5). True, before the Israelites established their monarchy, they were ruled by judges, one of whom was a woman, Deborah (Judges 4:4). But that appears to have been a one-off sort of deal, commanded by God for a specific reason at a particular time, not as a model for succeeding generations. Later, there was a Queen Athaliah, who for seven years alone ruled over the kingdom of Judah. But she established herself as monarch only by exterminating "all the offspring of the royal family" (2 Kings 11:1), so again she does not present a likely role model.

But as I cannot point out too often, we do not live in the ancient kingdom of Judah, nor do we live in a Jewish commonwealth literally governed by biblical law. The purpose of this book is to extract the philosophic principles that animate that law, not to apply them dogmatically or simplemindedly.

This too would be my response if I were challenged to explain certain apparent inconsistencies in my argument. For example, I've just faulted no-fault divorce. But doesn't the Hebrew Bible grant men wide leniency in divorcing their wives? Looked at from a different perspective, doesn't the New Testament generally forbid divorce, protecting men and women from abandonment? The specifically Christian Scriptures have, indeed, been interpreted as a challenge to Jewish patriarchy in the first century C.E., a time when Judean society was the most conservative in the Mediterranean world. In his role as social reformer, did not Jesus seem to downplay the centrality of the family, in contrast to the faith community? (See Mark 3:34–35, Matthew 10:35–37, Luke 14:26.)

These would all be valid objections to a different sort of book from this one. Since the Bible was written, or revealed, to address the needs of many societies in many eras, its philosophical framework is bound to be broad.

For us, what's imperative is not to deny women the opportunity to run for office because the Bible provides no model of female officeholders, nor to outlaw divorce, but merely to point out that women's natural power base is in the home, not in the office, the legislature, or the governmental executive's mansion, and that a wise society seeks to protect her power.

Even so, and even interpreted literally, the Bible adopts a more "modern" stance on women than you might expect. Its lyrical tribute to the ideal woman, in the last chapter of the book of Proverbs (31:10–31), paints a portrait of the "accomplished woman" as a most dynamic domestic entrepreneur. While her husband enjoys a quiet existence, deliberating with the other men before the city gate, "she is like a merchant's ship; from afar she brings her sustenance. She arises while it is yet night, and gives food to her household and a portion to her maidens. She envisions a field and buys it; from the fruit of her handiwork she plants a vineyard. With strength she girds her loins, and invigorates her arms. She discerns that her enterprise is good; her lamp is not snuffed out by night. She stretches out her hand to the distaff, and her palms support the spindle. She spreads out her palm to the poor, and extends her hands to the destitute. . . . She makes a cloak and sells [it], and delivers a belt to the peddler. . . . Give her the fruit of her hands; and let her be praised in the gates by her very own deeds."

This is truly "a woman in charge," if I may borrow the title of Carl Bernstein's 2007 biography of Mrs. Clinton. She is a powerful businesswoman, mixing with and commanding a variety of other people including men. Yet her enterprise is home-based, which makes all the difference.

The Bible wants us to appreciate that women have more power in the traditional role than they will have, in the long run, if the traditional family is undercut by a legal system uninformed by scriptural wisdom. Just such a legal system is what the Champion of Women, Senator Clinton, argues for. If God had a vote, He would not waste it supporting measures like the Paycheck Fairness Act or government-subsidized child care that, while appearing to be all about fairness and caring, in truth are about nothing other than luring more women into the workforce, which would sap their power, not add to it. Access to abortion and contraceptives similarly disempowers women, which is not what God with His vote would want to see happen. The freedom to make moral decisions at the individual level is a function of a healthy culture of strong families. That is the case even if the system and the culture are presided over, in the role of chief executive and commander in chief, by a woman.

4

Gay Marriage:
A Sacrifice for Molech

Asked on CNN if, as a Christian, he believed gays should have the right to marry, John Edwards tried to have it both ways: "No. Not personally," he said. "Now you're asking about me personally. But I think there's a difference between my belief system and what the responsibilities of the president of the United States are." He went on to say that his personal beliefs should play no role in how he would handle the issue as president.

Thanks to thinking like this, the idea of gay marriage has made startlingly swift political progress around the world, signaling what conservatives fear could turn into the beginning of the end of traditional ideas about marriage. Canada, Spain, South Africa, Belgium, and the Netherlands recognize the uniquely modern institution as they do marriage between a man and a woman. At present one U.S.

state, Massachusetts, distributes marriage certificates to same-sex couples. Eight other states, plus the District of Columbia, recognize "domestic partnerships" or "civil unions," which amount to recognizing gay marriage by another name. In other states and nations, the situation is fluid and no one knows how quickly the cause will advance.

Advocacy of same-sex matrimony may be heard loud and clear from the liberal wings of Christianity and Judaism alike. The Episcopal Church has been a trend leader among liberal denominations, threatening to tear apart the Angelican Communion. America as a whole seems split, with 58 percent opposing legal recognition of homosexual matrimony and 36 percent in favor, according to a June 2006 poll by ABC News.

In the Bible homosexual intercourse is a capital crime. Given what I said in Chapter 2 about how Scripture intends us to understand such heavy penalties—as teaching models, not legislative ones—you'll know right away that in a Bible-constitutional regime no gay people will be punished in any way. Yet the Bible's verdict on society's openly and legally embracing gay marriage would seem to be clear enough. Leviticus 18:22 certainly appears unambiguous on homosexuality: "You shall not lie with a man as one lies with a woman, it is an abomination."

In this chapter we will consider three classes of arguments used by religious liberals to justify their position. First of all, some argue that on same-sex relationships the Bible doesn't mean what it seems to mean. Second, others prefer to say that while the passages denouncing homosexual practice really do mean what they seem to mean, that fact shouldn't deter us from accepting the liberal view on the issue. Why? Because biblical teaching itself would even mandate that the troublesome verses may be disregarded. Third, another view admits that the Bible may reject same-sex love, but insists that we are justified in dismissing its view because nowadays we understand things about sexuality and society that the scriptural authors did not.

Of these, the view that denies the Bible's apparent meaning may seem the most unlikely. Some key passages that come up most often in the debate are from Genesis 2, Leviticus 20, Romans 1, and 1 Corinthians 6. I will quote here the familiar King James Version. In Genesis, God creates Adam, the first man, and then Eve from Adam's rib. Adam says of Eve, "This is now bone of my bones, and flesh of my flesh: she shall be called Woman, because she was taken out of Man." This prompts the narrator to comment, "Therefore shall a man leave his father and his mother, and shall cleave unto his wife: and they shall be one flesh." The text says nothing of man cleaving unto his husband. Leviticus, following upon the seeming proscription of homosexual relations, assigns a startlingly harsh penalty: "If a man also lie with mankind, as he lieth with a woman, both of them have committed an abomination: they shall surely be put to death; their blood shall be upon them."

In his letter to the Christian community in Rome, the apostle Paul decries the moral corruptions of pagan society, including this: "Even their women did change the natural use into that which is against nature. And likewise also the men, leaving the natural use of the woman, burned in their lust one toward another: men with men working that which is unseemly, and receiving in themselves that recompense of their error which was meet." In his letter to the Corinthians, Paul assails together a range of immoral lifestyles: "Know ye not that the unrighteous shall not inherit the kingdom of God? Be not deceived, neither fornicators, no idolaters, nor adulterers, *nor effeminate, nor abusers of themselves with mankind,* nor thieves, nor covetous, nor drunkards, nor revilers, nor extortioners, shall inherit the kingdom of God" (emphasis added).

Religious liberals insist that we are reading back into the text recent moral precepts that aren't really there. The Bible isn't forbidding homosexual intercourse of a loving, lawful, committed kind like that practiced in Massachusetts. It says nothing about such love! Rather it has in mind certain varieties of sexual exploitation that were cruel, unjust, unloving, and, needless to say, uncommitted. Regarding the Leviticus texts, about men lying "with mankind, as he lieth with a woman," one theory holds that it refers only to forbidden acts of ritual prostitution.

Another theory, advanced in the prestigious Anchor Bible commentary series by University of California–Berkeley scholar Jacob Milgrom, says that the Torah only has a problem with homosexual relations because the Bible wishes to keep reproduction and child-rearing within the bounds of a stable family. Why not let a gay couple marry and then adopt children? The sole objection there would be that the Bible doesn't have a concept of adoption. But now that adoption is a well-known and accepted institution, there should be no objection to a gay couple marrying and raising a family: if gay partners adopt children, they do not violate the *intent* of the prohibition in Leviticus.

Moving on to the New Testament, a Presbyterian minister, Jack Rogers, wrote a book called *Jesus, the Bible, and Homosexuality* (2006), telling how he once took a traditional, conservative view of the relevant biblical verses, and thus opposed the idea of the church giving its stamp of approval to homosexual relations. But after a closer look at the texts, he concluded that Paul had in mind not homosexuality per se but something more like cruising or serial random couplings in bathhouses. In *The Good Book: Reading the Bible with Mind and Heart* (1996), the gay Harvard minister Peter J. Gomes suggests that the sexual deviants Paul had in mind weren't gays and lesbians at all but rather "heterosexual people who performed homosexual acts." He doesn't say why Paul would go out of his way to admonish such people, who must be exceedingly rare.

The fact that so many divergent theories have been advanced indicates that something other than disinterested scholarship is at work. We observe here a mad and desperate dash by various writers, all eagerly seeking to reach the same conclusion—that the Bible's obvious meaning isn't its true meaning—but none in their collective haste being especially careful about how they get there. The passages are not obscurely phrased. The Hebrew Bible in particular has plenty of cryptic verses, but Leviticus 18:22 isn't one of them. Taken together, the texts in question are mutually reinforcing.

What about Paul's reinterpreters? In defending his position that Paul never took a stand on anything we would recognize today as gay relationships, Peter Gomes tries to show it wasn't Paul but the Church Fathers, a few generations after Paul, who took the hard line that only sex for procreation may be practiced by Christians. They did this because Paul (and Jesus) had preached that the end of the world was near. Why bring new lives into a world that wouldn't last long? When, contrary to expectations, the world didn't end, the Church Fathers decided that life must go on, which meant Christians having sex. But the approval for procreation was granted reluctantly. Hence Augustine's introduction of the ideal of sexual shame, and St. Thomas Aquinas's later formalization of the teaching against homosexuality. Writes Gomes, "the source again is not the Bible but the moral assumptions of the Church Fathers."

The problem with this is that it can't account for the rejection of homosexuality by Judaism, which never inherited the Church's dilemma when the world failed to end on schedule. The rabbis of the Talmud and Midrash who were Augustine's contemporaries not only clearly registered the Bible's teachings about homosexual intercourse but, on the basis of Scripture, warned of the dangers to a society that sought to legitimize gay sex by framing it in a fanciful same-sex marriage. The rabbis taught that when the Jews left Egypt and settled in the land of Canaan they encountered there a morally degenerate people, the Canaanites. One of that nation's corrupt practices was, in fact, to write marriage contracts for men with men and women with women. As the rabbis noted in the midrashic work *Sifra*, "A man would marry a man, and a woman [would marry] a woman." For such offenses, the Canaanites were justly "vomited out" of their land (Leviticus 18:25).

I suppose some other liberal Jewish clergyman will need to come along now and explain the circumstances that led the early teachers of his own faith to hallucinate a biblical proscription of homosexual relations, including homosexual marriage.

If it's not a hallucination, the next line of defense for gay marriage advocates—the second class of justifications—would be to concede that Scripture means what it seems to mean but to deny that, according to a broader conception of biblical values, the prohibition of sodomy is still relevant. There are two approaches: either to argue that the prohibition doesn't apply to non-Jews, or that it doesn't apply to Jews, Christians, or anyone else.

Commenting on the original text in Leviticus, the notorious verse 18:22—"You shall not lie with a man as one lies with a woman, it is an abomination"—Jacob Milgrom points out that it occurs in the context of specifically Jewish legislation. Thus the name of the intended recipient of the commandment against homosexual intercourse is Jews, not gentiles. Indeed, verse 18:20 warns married couples not to engage in sexual intercourse when the female partner is menstruating, a feature only of Jewish law.

One difficulty with this line of argument is that the Canaanites were a gentile society and their legal statutes, including gay marriage, resulted in their being jettisoned from their land. Another is that Leviticus 18 is also the prime biblical source for the prohibition of bestiality. If non-Jews are absolved of guilt for having relations with members of the same sex, they should also be free to be intimate with animals. Some gay marriage advocates would respond that, in biblical terms, there's an obvious difference between bestiality and homosexuality. The former is a moral offense, but the latter is merely a ritual one. And while the moral law given in the Torah may apply to non-Jews, the ritual law should not.

This defense hinges on how we interpret the Hebrew noun

toevah, or "abomination," which is the word that God in Leviticus chooses to describe what's wrong with homosexual intercourse. Gomes writes, "Homosexuality in Leviticus is condemned as ritually impure, the key to this conclusion being the fact that the word *abomination* does not usually describe something intrinsically evil, such as rape or theft, but something that is ritually impure, like eating pork or engaging in intercourse during menstruation." Just as Christians can eat pork without guilt, they may justifiably enjoy homosexual relations.

Sorry, no. In fact *toevah* designates a range of morally culpable acts. Gomes says it doesn't include things like theft. But on the contrary, it emphatically does. Deuteronomy forbids business fraud, the use of dishonest weights and measures, and comments: "For an abomination [*toevah*] of the Lord, your God, are all who do this, all who act corruptly" (25:16). The book of Proverbs uses the same term, *toevah,* to condemn corrupt business practices that certainly qualify as theft (11:1, 20:10, 20:23).

This mistake of liberal Christians seems to arise partly from an eagerness to grant homosexuals a religious seal of approval, but also from an unfamiliarity with the relevant biblical vocabulary in its original language.

Finally, some scriptural liberals simply feel they know better than the Bible. A liberal Reform rabbi, Yoel H. Kahn of San Francisco's Congregation Sha'ar Zahav, writes with admirable frankness on behalf of his colleagues in the Reform rabbinate: "Now, dissenting from Leviticus has not been an obstacle for us before"—so why should it now? His essay "The *Kedushah* [Holiness] of Homosexual Relations" is collected in gay blogger and journalist Andrew Sullivan's *Same-Sex Marriage, Pro & Con: A Reader.* Sullivan himself makes the point that there is no reason he should not be allowed to marry a partner, legally in the eyes of the state, when infertile heterosexual couples, or couples too old to reproduce, have that privilege. Traditionally, marriage has been linked with the creation of new life. Only a fertile man and a fertile woman can have a baby of their own. But the government does not make an issue of procreation in those cases. No matter how we interpret the Bible, what practical harm does it do if Sullivan and his boyfriend receive a marriage license?

Such questions lie at the heart of the third class of objections to religious conservatism as it pertains to homosexuality. It is not only arrogant people who would dismiss Leviticus 18:22 on moral and logical grounds. It's also men and women who earnestly ask themselves what the point of the moral stricture could be, and can think of none that is convincing.

Allow me to clarify. Marriage matters in its impact on both adults and on children. In the earlier history of our nation, Alexis de Tocqueville observed how religious and how free Americans were. He attributed this to marriage between a man and a woman. Simply put, a free people must be imbued with self-control. The alternative is tyranny, where citizens are disciplined not by themselves but by the state: "Religion is often unable to restrain man from the numberless temptations which chance offers; nor can it check that passion for gain which everything contributes to arouse; but its influence over the mind of woman is supreme, and women are the protectors of morals. There is certainly no country in the world where the tie of marriage is more respected than in America."

That last sentence breaks my heart. Tocqueville wrote it about America in 1831. Today the state of American marriage is extremely fragile, a fact with dire implications for the future of a free society.

Professor Stephanie Coontz writes in her recent book *Marriage, A History: How Love Conquered Marriage* that, as a social ideal, "it has become optional and more brittle." Indeed, "Between the 1970s and 1999 the number of unmarried couples living together in the United States increased sevenfold." Of this, the sorry decadence of American marriage, Coontz rightly sees the push for gay marriage as a symptom, "an inevitable result of the previous revolution in heterosexual marriage." But it is also more than that. It is a symptom that deepens the underlying illness. Gay marriage may be compared to a broken window on a city street. Civilization itself is fragile. One broken window is an invitation to more broken windows, more vandalism, descending ultimately to chaos. Smart city governments thus act quickly to check even minor acts of incivility.

A clue to the Bible's own reasoning on the issue may be found in the verse immediately preceding Leviticus 18:22. It refers to a pagan god and the horrific way in which he was worshipped, involving the immolation of children: "You shall not present any of your children to pass through for Molech, and do not profane the Name of your God—I am the Lord." Children were "passed through" a fire and sacrificed to Molech. The verse immediately following forbids homosexual relations.

The Bible doesn't order its verses as we would a grocery list, as items happen by chance to come to mind. Rather, it juxtaposes words and ideas in order to illuminate us about their interrelationship. Israel's Rabbi Shlomo Riskin makes this point about Leviticus 18:21–22. It is as if the first verse, warning against sacrificing the young and profaning God's name in the process, were the general principle of which the next verse is a practical application.

Certainly the honor and holiness of God's name are at stake in the gay marriage debate as it plays out between religious liberals and conservatives, both of whom claim the seal of God's approval for their preferred policies. More crucially, as the juxtaposed verses suggest, at stake is the future of children.

Since the 1960s, the ancient ideal of a child being raised by his committed, married parents has been terribly weakened. For many young couples, marriage no longer seems the obvious choice. There is hardly a stigma anymore to unwed domestic relationships, nor—as follows logically—to fathers skipping out on mothers, nor to mothers having children without a father's ever having been part of the household. Yet the need of a child for a mother and father remains. Every cultural development that changes the definition of marriage weakens the concept of marriage with children as a set, fixed ideal. It threatens to speed up the process of cultural breakdown that seems headed in the direction of making marriage an anachronism.

It is not the prospect of kids having gay parents that should worry us. Gay marriage will always be a sociologically minuscule phenomenon. It is the prospect of their having no parents, no linking of mother and father, no such unit demonstrating a commitment, for the sake of others, to overcoming the tensions that inevitably accompany the melding of male and female. To feed children into that fire—and in the name of religion, for goodness sake— is an abomination.

The religion of Molech today is one that insists that society subordinate its interests to the desires of individuals who, we are told, can't help but make the choices they do. A gay person is gay from birth or at least early childhood. That appears to be true. But from this, we are supposed to draw the inference that because he has no choice in his desires, he has no choice about his actions either. Because he has the desires, the actions must be accepted as well. Not only accepted, but embraced and endorsed by the culture, by the government. This is *tumah*-thinking, pure and simple.

With all this in mind, it seems safe to say that God's sympathies as a voter would be with those states—thirty-five in all at this writing—that have passed constitutional amendments or other laws barring the recognition of same-sex marriages. The time may come for a Federal Marriage Amendment to be added to the U.S. Constitution. Gay marriage, apart from its impact on children, comes down to the question we have seen again and again in this book as animating the debate between liberals and conservatives. Are people morally responsible for their actions? The faith of the Molech says, No, they can't help it. The faith of the Bible strongly disagrees.

5

Parenthood:
Here, Boy!

Here's a quick reality check for you, taking the form of a bumper sticker I saw on the back of a shiny black Ford Explorer in downtown Seattle. The sticker said, I VOTE FOR KIDS, and we can assume it didn't mean to indicate that the driver casts his election ballots for underage candidates. Nobody of any political persuasion would say that he votes AGAINST KIDS. Yet I had a strong hunch that the owner of the car was a liberal.

My reasoning was as follows. In the last chapter, we saw how closely linked the biblical objection to gay marriage is to God's concern about child-raising. We are, of course, not finished with the theme of parenthood. On a cluster of issues having to do not with homosexual but with heterosexual parents, liberals and secularists differ sharply from conservatives and religionists. The Bible, as always, not only provides a very general blueprint for governance, but also helps us map reality by explaining what at bottom it is—what single question—that divides the rival ideologies. In a nutshell, a biblical view sees children as transmitters of tradition. Secularism does not. This will have consequences for our biblical democracy, which will be a natalist regime. One consequence is that "voting for kids"—in other words, voting to fund government programs, presumably—is a liberal mantra rather than a conservative one, for the government cannot really help us transmit tradition to our children. That responsibility lies with parents.

As for that bumper sticker, I proceeded to confirm my suspicion by looking up online the organization that had printed it and that was identified in smaller type in its corner as the Every Child Matters Education Fund. While the group seeks to give the appearance of being nonpartisan, providing links to the campaign Web sites of all the Democratic and Republican 2008 contenders, I was struck by its legislative agenda. This was topped by demands addressed to President Bush and Congress to fund universal health care for kids on the model of Medicare, foster care, and increased preschool and after-school programs. There's nothing manifestly objectionable about any of those things. But compare the organization's priorities with that of a religiously conservative group like the Family Research Council. The latter is focused almost entirely on casting light over moral issues. As the FRC puts it, they would "protect families, schools, and places of worship against the cultural forces that threaten them, including biased and offensive media, pro-homosexual activism, and attacks on religious liberty." None of these things are accomplished by funding government programs. More often, the government itself is the danger, as we'll see in more detail in my chapter on education.

A theme in liberal rhetoric, as in conservative opinion, is indeed the defense of children. But defend them from what? Liberals focus on material threats, dangers to health or to other measures of physical well-being. The threat of global warming, say. Of secondhand smoke.

Or the peril posed by Oreo cookies. A *San Francisco Chronicle* story (May 12, 2003) quotes a California state senator and nutrition-reform advocate, Debra Bowen, who welcomed as a "good idea" a lawsuit seeking an injunction against Kraft Foods, which sells those terrifyingly lethal, trans fat–laced Oreos to innocent children. When Oreos are banned from sale to kids, just like cigarettes or liquor, then parents will be able to breathe easy.

Conservatives would be more worried about threats to moral innocence, as from TV, music, and other entertainment with questionable themes of a sexual nature. Conservatives also fret about undesirable influences exercised by public schools, which is why home-schooling has caught on among many who see keeping kids at home as the only way to save them from pernicious messages from teachers and other students. Those messages have to do, again, mostly with moral values. Liberals are usually much bigger believers in public school as a concept, though if there are too many minorities in the local school district, they will likely prefer private schools for their own children.

These are the dangers, from and to children, over which liberals and conservatives disagree. Let's try to sort them, looking for an underlying difference in attitude that drives all the other differences.

A good place to start is the contrasting values attached to having babies in the first place. The issues at stake in this chapter have as much to do with attitude and philosophy as they do with concrete policies. Consider the date of October 17, 2006, at 10:46 A.M., when officially according to the Census Bureau the U.S. population hit 300 million. There was no way to know who the 300 millionth American was. He or she could have been an arriving immigrant, but most people pictured a newborn baby.

Conservatives celebrated. Liberals were much more circumspect. The *San Francisco Chronicle* worried that "a growing population will force us to face innumerable challenges. . . . Americans are voracious consumers—we're eating up a quarter of the world's energy, developing our land at twice the rate of growth, and looking at big questions of water scarcity in the West—and our appetites are already producing strain on our resources and our qualify of life."

This was simply a more reserved way of saying what a biology professor at California State University at Fresno, Richard Haas, opined on the occasion: "Growth for growth's sake is the philosophy of the cancer cell."

Are more children a blessing or a cancer? Plenty of liberals would disagree with Professor Haas. Others would take issue only with the aggressiveness of his formulation. When our twin boys were born in Seattle, I reflected that my wife and I were registering an implicit dissent from the secular liberal value system of most Seattleites, as well as from that of the residents of America's other biggest left-leaning cities. These were our fourth and fifth kids. Our damp, tree-loving city is lushly green but largely sterile. In Seattle, which is America's second-most-childless city (just behind San Francisco), as well as being the chief metropolis of the country's most unchurched region (the Pacific Northwest), there are more dogs than kids.

The correlation between holding liberal political views and preferring not to reproduce has been noted by other writers, but not, I think, adequately explained. The data hold pretty consistently at the city and state level, juxtaposing the red-and-blue quilted electoral map of the 2004 election with information from the National Center for Health Statistics and the 2004 General Social Survey.

Liberal cities like Portland, Oregon, and Boston, and urban centers such as Manhattan have few children but lots of liberal Democrats. In 2004, writes Steve Sailer in *The American Conservative*, "[President] Bush carried the 19 states with the highest white fertility (just as he did in 2000), and 25 out of the top 26," while Democratic challenger John Kerry "won the 16 states at the bottom of the list." Professor Arthur Brooks, a scholar at Syracuse University's Maxwell School of Citizenship and Public Affairs, notes in *The Wall Street Journal* that "If you picked 100 unrelated politically liberal adults at random, you would find that they had had, between them, 147 children. If you picked 100 conservatives, you would find 208 kids. That's a 'fertility gap' of 41 percent."

Obviously, this must have something to do with the fact that conservatives are more likely to be traditionally religious. The thoughtful *New York Times* columnist David Brooks writes of a "spiritual movement" of "natalists," but offers no insight into why a spiritual perspective much more than a secular one would encourage reproduction. After all, secularists and liberals love their children too.

What accounts for the special conservative drive to reproduce? Could it be because traditional faiths proscribe contraception? But not all such religions do. Most Evangelical Christians have no problem with family planning. Nor do all believers follow the dictates of their faith. When it comes to birth control, American Catholics famously disagree with the strict rules of their church. Certainly, as I argue throughout this book, conservative culture is more imbued with scriptural values. And the Bible not only lends strong support to conservative beliefs, but takes an insistently strong pro-natalist stance. This could be part of the explanation we seek.

God likes babies. From the beginning of history as the Bible recounts it, He has been asking for more and more. "It is not good that man be alone," He observed while Adam was still the only human being on earth, thus counseling against celibacy (Genesis 2:18). Adam's descendant Noah, whose family alone survived the Deluge that engulfed the rest of humanity, was given the commandment of populating the world: "Be fruitful and multiply and fill the land" (9:1).

A person who has not yet reproduced is regarded as being in an unfinished state. Completion and fulfillment are dependent on having raised children. That's why the patriarch Abraham's wife, Sarah, chose to deal with her apparent inability to conceive by demanding that her husband sire offspring by Sarah's handmaid, Hagar. Sarah would adopt the resulting child. She instructed her spouse, "See, now, the Lord has restrained me from bearing; consort, now, with my maidservant, perhaps I will be built up through her" (16:2). Evidently, adoption is considered a significant alternative to biological parenthood.

Sarah did eventually have a child of her own, Isaac. Rebecca, Isaac's wife, was also seemingly barren and "entreated the Lord" for children along with Isaac (25:21). God granted their prayerful wish. Their son Jacob's wife, Rachel, was, again, barren at first and deemed this a cause of extreme anguish. "Give me children—otherwise I am dead," she told Isaac.

Nor was it merely the idiosyncratic wish of these patriarchs and matriarchs to have children. If we move forward in history to the period of the Hebrew prophets, we find Isaiah teaching that God made the world with reproduction uppermost in His mind: "He is the God, the One Who fashioned the earth and its Maker; He established it; He did not create it for emptiness; He fashioned it to be inhabited" (45:18).

This is the view of the Hebrew Bible. By contrast, the Christian Scriptures are ambivalent about marriage, which would imply a different view of the reproductive imperative. That makes sense because the earliest Christians assumed, with the Messianic era having already begun, the world was about to end.

Jesus considered celibacy a worthy lifestyle for some: "There are eunuchs who have made themselves eunuchs for the sake of the kingdom of heaven. He who is able to receive this, let him receive it" (Matthew 19:12). The apostle Paul went further: "To the unmarried and the widows I say that it is well for them to remain single as I do.

But if they cannot exercise self-control, they should marry. For it is better to marry than to be aflame with passion" (1 Corinthians 7:8–9). But Christians have on this point mostly reverted to the Hebraic worldview.

Having established Scripture's natalism, we are still left uncertain of exactly why biblical religion favors reproduction. I think this points to a fundamental difference between the biblical and secular worldviews about what children are for in the first place.

Of course, many secularists do have children. If you asked them why they choose to do so, and with enthusiasm that needn't be any less than that of their religious neighbors, they would say things like: "I love children." "I want to give my love to a child or children." "I want to nurture a human being, and see him grow and thrive." These are all beautiful and sincere sentiments. But let us be honest and see that not one of them would be unexpected coming from a would-be pet owner looking for a dog, cat, rabbit, or turtle to buy and care for.

By this I intend no offense. I know liberals would give their lives for their kids, though so would some pet owners for their pets. But the absence of an additional religious imperative for child-raising makes it understandable that liberals reproduce less often. Just as pet ownership is optional, so too is having children if the only reasons for doing so are those cited above. It's also possible to have too many pets, and neighbors will be justified in chastising you for this. Thus a staple of local newsgathering, often posted on Internet roundup sites like the Drudge Report, is the eccentric person with way too many pets: There was the couple in Aliso Viejo, California, who had eighty-two cats, which were seized and taken away by authorities. There was the lady in Clearwater, Florida, with a hundred cats, which led police to condemn her house as a public nuisance. There was the man in Ocala, Florida, charged with animal cruelty for keeping three hundred cats. And so on.

In the same way, families with five or more children can expect to be reproached periodically by strangers in supermarkets and on sidewalks, wanting to know, "Don't you think you've had enough already?" Friends of mine out for a hike in a state park on Orcas Island north of Seattle, with their *three* well-behaved children, were accosted by another hiker, a single man, who sneered, "Have you considered birth control?" The question, or one like it, is typically delivered in the same tone of voice with which the very same people (undoubtedly) would question someone with a lit cigarette in his mouth: "Do you mind?" "Do you have to smoke that thing?" My brother-in-law and his wife in Jerusalem have eighteen children. Someday, I would be curious to take him and his family for a walk on the sidewalks of Seattle and see what happens.

The religiously motivated are undeterred by secular scolding because, unlike liberalism and secularism, a biblical worldview sees children as having an additional role besides that of the recipient of parental affection and government nurturance. These adorable little tykes have the glorious task of being transmitters of an ancient tradition to posterity. Without them, the tradition perishes. Having a child is like establishing an Internet cable link with the future of mankind. The Bible teaches this most notably in connection with the Exodus from Egypt. "And you shall tell your son on that day, saying 'It is because of this that the Lord acted on my behalf when I left Egypt' " (Exodus 13:8).

"And it shall be when your son will ask you at some future time, 'What is this?' you shall say to him, 'With a strong hand the Lord removed us from Egypt from the house of bondage' " (13:14).

Educating children as transmitters is the parental role that subsumes all others. Nothing else a parent might do is commanded in such sweeping terms, a responsibility without limit in time or place. In Deuteronomy, in Moses's farewell speech to the Jews before he dies and they enter the land of Israel, the Lawgiver advises: "And these matters that I command you today shall be upon your heart. You shall teach them thoroughly to your children and you shall speak of them while you sit in your home, while you walk on the way, when you retire and when you arise" (6:6–7). For this reason, just as your Internet access depends on countless other computers being linked to yours, the link between generations—between parents and teachers and children as students—is stronger depending on how many children you have.

We can now understand those apparently unrelated issues that I noted at the beginning of this chapter. It is perfectly consistent that conservatives would rejoice at the 300 millionth American, pictured as a freshly born infant in a hospital somewhere, while liberals would have their joy damped by terrors about that baby's presumed appetite for physical resources. For conservatives, the baby was another link with our moral future. For liberals, the 300 millionth American was like the three hundredth cat owned by the man in Ocala, Florida.

Similarly, conservatives worry about moral threats more than material ones because the mission entrusted to children is a moral one. Liberals worry about global warming, secondhand smoke, or partially hydrogenated vegetable oil in Oreo fillings because children have no role as conveyors of a moral tradition.

Finally, conservatives would be more likely to homeschool their kids. That's for two reasons. First, because in a public school setting parents have little control over the curriculum's moral content. Second, very possibly, because of the Bible's stated preference for parents educating their own children rather than handing off the responsibility to others. Parents *are* responsible, capable as individuals of making the right educational choices for their young ones. The Bible envisions no school system, no professional teachers, at all.

It's no surprise, then, that parenting divides those Americans who are most influenced by the biblical ethos from those who are least influenced by it. The survival of the biblical understanding of reality is dependent, quite simply, on religious people having kids.

In the struggle between rival worldviews that characterizes modern times, the biblical view is seemingly on the ropes, under constant attack from secularism. You could have one kid and teach him really well. If he grows up imbued with your values and passes them on to his one own single child, that's a good thing. But just as in war, the number of soldiers on the ground matters no less than the qualities of the combatants. The relevance of this to a religion's future is illustrated nowhere more starkly than in my own Jewish community, where fertility is clearly impacted by worldview. As the statisticians Antony Gordon and Richard M. Horowitz have shown, every 100 Reform Jews, associated with the most secular-leaning Jewish denomination, will within four generations be reduced to only 10 Jews. Every 100 Conservative Jews, another liberal denomination, will be reduced to 29. Yet a group of 100 Orthodox Jews will increase, in four generations, either to 434 or 3,401, depending on whether they are Centrist Orthodox or Hasidic/Yeshiva Orthodox.

Liberalism acts as a powerful acid on the existence of future generations. Conservatism, as a powerful preservative. In the culture war, that simple fact will have far-reaching consequences, happy ones from a biblical point of view.

Less happy, perhaps, is the conclusion we are left with that God might not, after all, vote for kids. Not that He would vote against them. However, He would cast His ballot against politicians who, even if they don't share the arch-secularist aversion to populating the planet, express their genuine concern for children mainly through calling for more government programs, thus demonstrating that they have missed the point of what most pointedly threatens the young in their role as transmitters of tradition to posterity. Rather than "for kids," God would vote for adults who appreciate the true importance of the next generation.

6

Abortion:
A Litmus Test

More than perhaps any other issue, abortion ought to serve as a litmus test in American public life, allowing us to gauge the degree to which a candidate feels comfortable with the politics of God. In this respect the candidacy of Rudolph Giuliani, a favorite with Jewish neoconservatives, is telling. Giuliani is frankly pro-choice yet neocons prefer to focus on his credentials as a counter to "Islamofascism." Those on the Right inclined to look to the Bible for guidance would point out that in a struggle of civilizations, that of the West against Islamic terror, the West can count on losing if we don't have God on our side, and of that, where we come down on the abortion question is a useful indicator. We'll come back to this point in Chapter 20.

What sets abortion apart from the other political issues is that advocates on either side so clearly differ about no less weighty a question than the proper place of God in the governing of our public lives. The only convincing arguments against abortion are religious ones, assuming as they do that at some point a spiritual reality, a soul, is infused in the unborn within the womb. Were it not for that assumption, extinguishing the life of the fetus would pose no great moral challenge.

You might make the same argument about, say, gay marriage. There is certainly no convincing purely secular argument against recognizing same-sex unions. Yet plenty of people, especially men, who don't care a fig about God would revolt at the idea of the government giving its seal of approval to the marriage of John and Jack, simply because of the overwhelming "yuck" factor.

However, even having concluded in the previous chapter that the Bible is philosophically natalist in orientation—that is, it's pro-baby—we would still not be justified in drawing an easy conclusion on how our biblical government would handle the question of legal abortion. That question is not easy, in fact, in the least. It's hard to avoid the conclusion that neither of the two extreme positions in the abortion debate has based its view on a close reading of the Bible. A true scripturally based position would be classified as pro-life, with a definite hard-edged quality, yet also with what may seem a surprising nuance of its own.

Among those Americans who would prefer the government to allow maximum liberty to women in disposing of their pregnancy as they see it, one finds a community of the so-called "Pious and Pro-choice." That was the headline of a July 30, 2006, *Boston Globe* article that sought to cast in a flattering light a broad coalition of liberal religious denominations that favor abortion rights. A liberal rabbi, Dennis S. Ross, on the Planned Parenthood Clergy Advisory Board, assures abortion practitioners and other pro-choice partisans on the group's Web site, "When it comes to abortion, the Bible cannot be used to justify an anti-abortion position because the Bible is silent on the issue."

Meanwhile, at the most restrictive end of the spectrum of views on abortion, one finds the position of the Catholic Church. In his 1995 encyclical *Evangelium Vitae* ("The Gospel of Life"), Pope John Paul II calls abortion an act of "deliberate and direct killing, by whatever means it is carried out, of a human being in the initial phase of his or her existence, extending from conception to birth.

"The moral gravity of procured abortion is apparent in all its truth if we recognize that we are dealing with murder."

Is abortion "murder"? And if so, does that description apply through the whole length of pregnancy, from the moment of conception on? John Paul cites a previous Church teaching that invokes "modern genetic science" to show that "from the first instant there is established the program of what this living being will be: a person, this individual person with his characteristic aspects already well determined. Right from fertilization the adventure of a human life begins." Since the software in the cell, DNA, has already been written from the moment egg joins with sperm and the unique genetic data are determined, there is an integrity that unites the physical being of an individual human, from this moment of conception through gestation to birth and into childhood, adolescence, adulthood, old age, and death. To kill this individual at any point along the way is then the very same act of "murder."

One hesitates to argue with the pope. In fact, from personal experience I hesitate to give what I understand to be the biblical view on this question at all. That is because I know how fraught with emotion, and pain, it is for many women, also for men, including friends of mine. And no doubt for many readers of this book. In the United States currently, the ratio of abortions to live births is about 25 to

100. That's almost 1.3 million abortions a year. I remember from my days as an unmarried man living in New York City, sitting in a restaurant with a smart and opinionated girl, talking about issues of the day. Somehow, abortion came up and I flatly stated my opinion that it seemed to be murder. What an idiot I was not to think of the possible personal ramifications for the young woman across the table from me. She started to cry and very quickly it became clear that, though our meals had just been served, we had to leave the restaurant.

With that preliminary having been stated, wouldn't it be surprising if the Bible really said nothing about abortion, one way or the other?

Admittedly, the choice of relevant scriptural texts is slim, and not all those that are noted by abortion foes as being relevant actually are so. For example, Jeremiah opens his book with God's attestation to him, "Before I formed you in the belly I knew you, and before you left the womb I sanctified you; I established you as a prophet unto the nations" (1:5). But this could as well mean that he was exceptional—which clearly he was. God conceived of Jeremiah, his personality and his role in the drama of religious history, even before his mother conceived him. Would this be true of anyone? If so, that is not obvious from the text.

In the beautiful story told in Luke's gospel, Mary, pregnant with Jesus, goes to visit her cousin Elizabeth, who is pregnant with the future John the Baptist. Upon hearing Mary's greeting, the baby in Elizabeth's womb does a somersault: "For, lo, as soon as the voice of your salutation sounded in my ears, the babe leaped in my womb for joy" (1:44). But again, it could easily be argued that we are talking, by definition, about two extraordinary babies, from whose miraculous behavior general rules about fetal personhood cannot be drawn.

A liberal Bible interpreter, meanwhile, could confront us with the most troubling passage for the pro-life cause, Exodus 21:22–25, which has the merit of being a legal text. It tells what should happen in the case of an accidental abortion.

Here is the scenario: Two men are fighting. One of them collides violently with a pregnant woman. She then "miscarries." If, apart from the miscarriage, no "fatality" (*ason*) occurs—meaning, the mother survives—then a civil penalty is imposed. The man who did it pays a fine. Only if there is a "fatality" is there the possibility of more serious penalties. Now, in biblical law, an accidental killing, manslaughter, is punished with exile. If abortion were regarded as killing a human being with full rights to legal protection like any other person, our accidental abortionist should also be subjected to exile. But he is not. Seemingly, it follows that if the abortion were committed with intent, assuming the mother was not killed in the process, it could not be treated as murder any more than any other ordinary case of assault would be.

The difficulty with this passage for our purposes is that the phrase often translated as "and she miscarries" (*v'yatzu y'ladeha*) literally means "and her children come out." (Oddly, the idiom is phrased in the plural.) This could mean the baby dies. Or it might only mean a premature live birth. In this more literal reading, the "fatality" mentioned in the text could be that of the mother or the baby. If neither dies as a result of the accident, the careless pugilist only pays a fine. The passage from Exodus has rightly been called enigmatic. It reminds us of the need for an ancient and authoritative tradition of interpretation.

Which brings us to the verse that I think addresses our question most directly. Again, what is required is a literal reading. Is abortion ever considered murder? Though liberal Jewish groups, I'm sorry to say, like to cover this up, the rabbis of the Talmud, contemplating America in the opening decade of the twenty-first century, would say that hundreds of thousands of such murders are being committed by

Americans against unborn babies every year. The Talmud points to a verse in Genesis, a verse that appropriately is also the source for explaining what is so wrong with murder in the first place.

It appears in the context of God's instructions to Noah and his sons. They have just exited the Ark on which they and their families rode out the great storm that destroyed all human and animal life. God is explaining to them how they will go about rebuilding civilization, in the course of which He directs them to take note of a general principle: "Whoever sheds the blood of man, by man shall his blood be shed; for in the image of God He made man" (Genesis 9:6). That's how the verse is conventionally translated. Rabbi Yishmael, in the Talmud's tractate *Sanhedrin* (57b), notes that the Hebrew literally says, "Whoever sheds the blood of a person [who is] inside another person (*ba'adam*), his blood shall be shed." The key Hebrew preposition here, *"ba,"* almost always means "in" or "inside" not "by." The noun *"adam"* is a generic designation for a person, not necessarily a male, or for humanity as a whole.

The only "person inside another person" we know of is the baby in its mother's womb. To shed the blood of that baby is for the descendants of Noah—that is, mankind—a capital crime.

However, does this mean that abortion is murder from conception on? No, it doesn't. Notice the second phrase in the verse we've just looked at: "Whoever sheds the blood of a person [who is] inside another person, his blood shall be shed; *for in the image of God He made man*" (emphasis added). This tells us why murdering the baby in the womb deserves such a harsh punishment. In some way that you would have to be a mystic to really understand, God imprinted His image on the face of man. There is a glow, an effulgence, an aura about a human being that we receive from the Lord. To prematurely extinguish it represents a grave crime.

But when does it initially appear on the countenance of an embryo, a fetus?

A human embryo graduates to the status of a fetus at the end of the eighth week (fifty-six days) of gestation. Talmudic teaching regards the embryo through to its fortieth day as possessing no claim on personhood (*Niddah* 30a). The Catholic Church held much the same belief from the thirteenth through the nineteenth centuries, basing its view on that of Aristotle, who held that the male received a "rational soul" at forty days of gestation while the female was similarly endowed with a soul at eighty days. The Talmud also preserves a tradition, rejected as a matter of practice but still interesting, that makes exactly the same distinction: the male becomes a person at forty days, the female at eighty days.

These seemingly arbitrary numbers are alluded to in the Bible. The book of Leviticus (12:1–5) defines a waiting period following delivery of a baby, during which the mother recovers from the experience of pregnancy and birth. She may not enter the Temple in Jerusalem and is subject to other religious restrictions. The period ends after forty days from the birth of a baby boy, eighty days from the birth of a girl. The waiting period recapitulates the time when the embryo awaited its being imbued with a soul. The most sensible interpretation is that the boy or girl achieves personhood at forty days of gestation, but there are other reasons—beyond the scope of our brief discussion—why the mother of the baby girl must wait eighty instead of forty days before resuming all normal activities.

Certainly, from a medical perspective, the figure of forty days is not arbitrary. For those forty days, an embryo is sexually ambiguous, with a reproductive system that is undifferentiated as to being male or female. After forty days, depending on the Y chromosome's presence or absence, the embryo develops respectively as either a male (with testes) or a female (with ovaries). Personhood is dependent on sexual differentiation. If you are a woman, can you imagine yourself as a man? If you are a man, can you imagine yourself as a woman? Not easily, I assume. Also by forty days, all essential organs

have started to form. The limbs begin to move spontaneously, as ul-
trasound can detect. We now are in the presence of a human being.
Before forty days, the person is only potential.

Some opinions, religious and otherwise, would forbid and criminalize abortion from conception on because—so the argument goes—
in the context of the developing human life, potential and actual are
a meaningless distinction. The conservative journalist Ramesh Pon-
nuru expresses this in secular terms in his book *The Party of Death:
The Democrats, the Media, the Courts, and the Disregard for Human Life* (2006).

"All of us who read this page were once human embryos. The history of our bodies began with the formation of the embryo. *We
were* those embryos, just as we were once fetuses, infants, children,
and adolescents. But we were never a sperm cell and an egg cell.
(Those cells were genetically and functionally parts of other human
beings.) The formation of the embryo marks the beginning of a new
human life: a new and complete organism that belongs to the human species."

While this sounds reasonable, the Bible doesn't support Pon-
nuru's idea that the body is the person. We are created in the image
of God, which is what gives us the exalted status of persons. But His
image is not imprinted on us the moment the history of the body begins. That is the message of the verses in Genesis, Chapters 1 and 2,
that describe God's creation of man. It was a two-part process: first
a living body, then a living soul.

In Part One, God brought forth "living creatures" (*nefesh
chayah*), comprising all sorts of animals including man, whose
physiology is animal in nature (Genesis 1:24–25). This step in the
creation process is described a chapter later (2:7) in slightly different
terms: "And the Lord formed the man of dust from the ground, and
He blew into his nostrils the soul of life; and man became a living

creature (*nefesh chayah*)." In Part Two, which unfolds in the Garden of Eden, God takes the raw living material of animal "man" and performs a special act of creation, imprinting the man with His image: "So God created man in His image, in the image of God He created him; male and female He created them" (1:27).

Thus, two separate creations, body and soul. This is the reading of Rabbi Obadiah Sforno (1475–1550), but it is also apparent from a careful consideration of the text.

This two-part creation process is recapitulated in gestation. The history of the body begins at conception. The history of the soul in the body, the image of God impressed upon the body, begins at forty days. Because the Bible defines murder as the crime that defaces the divine image in man, it follows that to kill the potential life, the *nefesh chayah*, in the womb on day thirty-nine is not murder. It is not a capital crime in biblical terms.

But an act doesn't have to be murder to be wrong. To speak of the "murder" of a week-old embryo is not justified, either from a biblical or a commonsense perspective. We might, incidentally, apply the same analysis to the debate about government-funded bioresearch using embryonic stem cells, which entails destroying the embryo (a four- to five-day-old blastocyst, comprising fifty to one hundred cells in all) well short of the forty-day mark. That doesn't mean, however, that either of these things is a matter of moral indifference. This is notwithstanding the view of Democratic House Speaker Nancy Pelosi, who cheered for increased funding for embryonic stem cell research, saying, "Science is a gift of God to us all, and science has taken us to a place that is biblical in its power to cure." Uh-huh. In fact, the Bible has another relevant category of sin, the wasting of human seed.

Scripture cares that we not treat lightly the miracle of procreation. Later in Genesis, Chapter 38, the Bible tells the story of two brothers, Er and Onan. When Er died childless, custom indicated that Onan was obliged to marry Er's widow, Tamar. Any children born in the marriage of Onan and Tamar would be attributed, mystically, not to Onan as father but to Er. However, Onan chose selfishly and impiously to practice coitus interruptus. Instead of impregnating his wife, he spilled his seed on the ground. God found this to be evil, and killed Onan for it. Hence the term "onanism," applied loosely to masturbation.

Ending a pregnancy from conception on *may* be murder depending on the circumstances. But *at any stage* it is certainly and always the sin of Onan—not a crime in the sense of an act punishable by a human court, but still a moral offense. Just as no one would propose to criminalize masturbation or premature withdrawal during intercourse, the Bible would not recommend regulating abortion except once the embryo has become a person. By the same token, to destroy a five-day-old embryo for the purpose of deriving a line of stem cells from it might be justified on narrow legal grounds. At the same time, denying government funding to embryonic stem cell research seems reasonable as a way of encouraging scientists to develop other stem cell sources that do not entail destroying embryos at all.

We are left with abortion as a moral outrage whenever it is committed, but a punishable offense, subject to criminal penalties, only from the fortieth day on. This would not sit well, it seems, with either the extreme pro-life or the extreme pro-choice forces. Especially not so, it has to be admitted, with the latter.

That much is clear from Scripture. Even before looking at the biblical text, however, we see that a purely pro-choice view conforms to the counterscriptural worldview that I have been developing throughout this book, that sees men and women as entrapped in nature, not fully free to resist the demands of the body. Abortion as birth control can represent an implicit claim by the woman that she couldn't help herself, couldn't say no to a desired sexual coupling. Because she couldn't resist, she is given the opportunity to end the resulting pregnancy. You see, our animal nature is such that we need this if-all-else-fails measure.

Regulating abortion assumes the opposite, that a couple is not compelled by nature to have sex (or to have unprotected sex). If a woman gets pregnant, certainly outside the rare context of rape, she can be held responsible for her action. That means she goes through with the pregnancy.

Currently, of course, the 1973 Supreme Court decision *Roe v. Wade* tightly constrains American lawmakers from regulating abortion. *Roe* makes it all but impossible to criminalize abortion even up to the moment of birth. If *Roe* is overturned and the power to make laws about abortion restored to the process of state-level democratic decision-making, that will present a welcome opportunity to construct biblically informed anti-abortion laws. In our biblical America, I wouldn't expect any state to make this terrible procedure a capital offense, but for the abortion provider serious penalties would be appropriate. The compromise suggested here will, I hope, be considered.

But if it's not? How would God vote, for the pro-choice candidate who favors a strong hand in dealing with Islamofascism? Or for the pro-life candidate who would hesitate to exercise the neocon option of bombing Iran and might lack some of the hard-edged, foreign policy savvy of, let's say, a Giuliani-esque character? I offer no endorsement. Yet if our quest to bring God more directly into American political life means anything at all, it must surely demand setting down certain definite tests of a politician's acceptability. Abortion, I believe, is one of those. A candidate who fails the test really doesn't "get it," and could be supported only with the greatest reluctance.

7

Education:
If God Ran for School Board

S ince education is mostly a local rather than a federal matter, we
are compelled here to abandon the realm of national politics
and dive down deep to the much smaller dimensions of the city
school district and the state board of ed. In the Seattle suburb where
I live, as in many other places across the country, candidates for the
school board put out signs, stuck in the ground along the main drag
that runs down the center of our slender island in the middle of
Lake Washington. A winning candidate will include some idealistic-
sounding but otherwise meaningless slogan under her name: CHIL-
DREN FIRST, or similar. If God ran for school board, what would
His slogan be?

Like other family-related issues, education under our biblical
democratic-pluralist regime may call up frightening images for

some. Picture the return of school prayer, for example, which would only be an option in school districts even if the Supreme Court reversed itself. Imagine children invited each morning in their homeroom class to praise a generic, nondenominational deity, politely requesting "God Almighty" to bless them in their studies along with their teachers and parents.

This was the scenario in New York public schools that provided the Supreme Court with the 1962 case (*Engel v. Vitale*), resulting in school prayer being banned nationally as unconstitutional. A decision a year later, *Abington School District v. Schempp,* resulted in the banning of school Bible readings. Were either practice to be revived in some locality today, liberals would ask us to imagine the psychological impact on the little atheist child, or the little Zen Buddhist child who doesn't believe in a theistic deity, or the little Hindu child who does not confine herself to belief in one god alone, or the little Jewish child who fears that when his Christian classmates say "God" they are really thinking of Jesus Christ. Woe and pity upon this delicate and vulnerable young person, who may feel . . . uncomfortable!

Actually, no matter how we envision the reform of public school education, things could hardly be any worse than they are now. In his five-hundred-year narrative of Western cultural decline, *From Dawn to Decadence,* historian Jacques Barzun traces the course of "school decay" back to the development of certain inane pedagogical theories. "The great 19th century invention, the public school, had lost the power to make children literate. Methods useless for that purpose, absurd teacher training, the dislike of hard work, the love of gadgetry, and the efforts to copy and to change the outer world ruined education throughout the West."

Teachers were steadily losing their authority to teach, or giving it up—in a sinister parallel with the way parents too were in the process of losing their own sense of authority. Probably, this erosion of adult self-confidence can be attributed to religion's fall from its own pedestal of authority, which it had occupied until the nineteenth century. Adults once felt they could impart to children certain basic truths about morality and its author, God. With the rise of Darwinism and other challenges to ancient beliefs, faith lost confidence in itself, and so, accordingly, did parents and teachers.

Meanwhile sexual liberation ideology injected further havoc. Barzun writes, "The great damage from the sexual emancipation occurred in the public school, where sexual talk and behavior, being tolerated, distracted from work. The resulting early pregnancies caused disaster of all kinds. But so great was the thrall of the sexual that school authorities dealt with the problem by means of courses, free contraceptives, and handbooks giving a full view of the subject, its variants and aberrations."

In this context, what reforms would a biblical worldview suggest, and would they not be revealed inevitably as futile? After all, cultural observers are beginning to realize that children are not programmable computers. It is not the case that if you set a child with no commendable values down in a school and then ask his teachers to instruct him about proper values, he will absorb the teaching like a computer that has just had installed the latest software update. A human being's consciousness is shaped much more by experience than by instruction. That's why it has been found that teachers trying to impress young people with the virtues of sexual abstinence, or of contraception, are equally ineffective. That is, they are ineffective in the absence of a home life that already predisposed the child to responsible behavior from a much earlier age.

The Bible, of course, knew all this thousands of years ago. That is why most education in the ideal scriptural society would devolve not on schools, public or private, but on parents. I mentioned this in an earlier chapter. The Pentateuch is repetitive to the point of exhaustion with instructions about pedagogy that place the responsibility firmly, exclusively on the parent: "so that you may relate in the ears of your son and your son's son" (Exodus 10:2), "And you shall tell your son on that day" (13:8), "make them known to your children and your children's children" (Deuteronomy 4:9), "Ask your father and he will relate it to you, your elders and they will tell you" (32:7). So too the moralizing book of Proverbs: "Hear, my child, the discipline of your father, and do not forsake the teaching of your mother" (1:8), "Heed, my son, the command of your father, and do not forsake the teaching of your mother" (6:20), and so on.

In this ideal society, home-schooling would be the norm. The reasons for this include the moral responsibility that teaching your kids puts on you. Handing them over to a school where you have no say in what is taught relieves you of the possibility of making the sort of free will choices that the biblical worldview sees as the glory of the human being. It is altogether too easy. It also reinforces the teaching of *tumah* that you, despite being an adult, are incapable of making the right choices for your children, instructing them well. That's a destructive idea for adults no less than for kids.

Perhaps more worrisome, as soon as a corporate entity, the government, is entrusted with young people's education, the temptation is to shape them according to a man-made ideology. Aristotle in his *Politics* lamented that his Greek fellow citizens had no school system. Believing that the citizen belongs to the state, not to himself, the philosopher insisted that "education must be one and the same for all, and that the responsibility for it must be a public one, not the private affair which it is now, each man looking after his own children and teaching them privately whatever private curriculum he thinks they ought to study." Parents are not suited to hold such authority over their own children. In comparatively modern times, the seventeenth-century scientist and educator John Amos Comenius proposed a state-financed system of universal education in which kids would be indoctrinated with a new religion of science, "Pansophia." In recognition of his educatory theorizing, he was offered the first presidency of Harvard College but turned it down. In the nineteenth century, "the father of American public education,"

Horace Mann, saw it as the role of schools to inculcate a certain "public philosophy."

Shall we get rid of public schools? No, for we live not in that scriptural utopia but in the real world, where many parents have to work long hours that preclude the home as a venue for anything like serious instruction. Indeed, the first nation to be formed by the biblical ethos reached this conclusion about the impracticality of universal home education. According to biblical historians, there were probably schools in ancient Israel from the period of the monarchy—David's kingdom—onward, but these institutions were probably informal, certainly not universal or mandatory. The Talmud tells, however, how the Jewish nation instituted a public school system, the first of its kind in the world, about three decades after the life of Jesus, in the time of Jerusalem's Second Temple shortly before the holy city was destroyed by Roman forces.

For centuries, the Jews had interpreted very literally the phrase in Deuteronomy (11:19), "And you shall teach them to your children to discuss them"—namely, teach the Bible's laws. Due to a grammatical oddity, a literal reading could be, "And you *yourselves* shall teach your children."

However, when the nation's leaders realized that some students were not receiving a proper education, they instituted a series of reforms. First a school system was set up in Jerusalem, then in the provinces for high-school-age youths. Finally, the high priest Joshua ben Gamla "enacted that [local authorities] should install teachers of children in every district and town, and they should bring in [children] of ages six or seven" and up to be taught (*Baba Batra* 21a).

The system was publicly funded and compulsory. The year was 64 C.E., meaning that it was a short-lived experiment since Judea was laid waste six years later by the Romans. Not for another nineteen centuries would a country, the United States, undertake such an enterprise. As Joshua ben Gamla realized, given the realities of life, public schools are probably the best way to ensure quality education

for the greatest number of children. They are here to stay, and there's
no point in enlightened believers in the Bible denying this.

Yet the Bible would offer some discrete ideas for improving the
system we have, along with a more fundamental challenge. The
smaller suggestions first:

Bring back corporal punishment. The book of Proverbs is very
keen on our not forgetting the essential aid offered by the judicious
use of physical chastisement to establish authority. It also reminds
us that there is no contradiction between spanking a child and caring for and loving him. On the contrary, "One who spares his rod
hates his child, but he who loves him disciplines him in his youth"
(13:24). This is God's way with us, his own children: "For the Lord
admonishes the one He loves, and like a father He mollifies the
child" (3:12).

Consider instituting separate schools for boys and girls. In the
Temple where Jesus worshipped, women and men were separated,
as the Psalm indicates in an indirect fashion: "Praise the Lord," we
are advised, "young men and also maidens, old men together with
youths" (148:12). The young men are separated from maidens by the
subtle hint of the word "also," while the old men are gathered together with young men. This was done on the theory that sex dis-
tracts us. Actually it is not a theory, but a readily evident observation
from everyday life, confirmed by a genre of "small" news stories, not
infrequently reported, about high school students and younger kids
engaging in sexual acts in the classroom, sometimes with class going
on. I know that's not the norm in your local suburban high school,
but the distraction inherent in a situation where young people are
cast together, the girls barely clothed, should be obvious to all.
Schools separated by gender would diminish this problem in a
stroke.

*Consider the European system of separate tracks based on career
goals.* In the Scriptures, perhaps the wisest word to educators and
the least heeded is again in the book of Proverbs: "Train the youth

according to his way; even when he grows old, he will not swerve from it" (22:6). This means that every young person has a distinctive set of abilities and inclinations. According to current cultural assumptions, at least in the suburbs where I live, every single kid has to be on college-prep track; otherwise his parents will be compelled to hang their heads in shame. The Bible points out to us the absurdity of imposing our own daydreams and wish fulfillments on a child without regard to the direction urged on him by his own personality, his own soul. The myth that university must be a universal experience is one we would do well to jettison. Much better to allow children to decide for themselves whether they need a liberal education or a technical one, and direct schools to prepare them accordingly for either.

What about school prayer, or class Bible readings? Before rendering a verdict, we need to appreciate a big truth. It is that from the 1960s on, not only was the old biblical America being dismantled—the Supreme Court in the decisions mentioned above was only following the zeitgeist—but a new America was being erected in its place, the institutionalized secularism that controls our public schools. If God ran for school board, his slogan would be: BREAK THE SECULAR-THEOCRATIC MONOPOLY.

Yes, secularism is a religion, and as such, should probably be capitalized. Many individuals who identify nominally as Jews or Christians in fact are devout secularists. All this would be fine—after all, America is a big country with plenty of room for every spiritual predilection—but for the tendency of secularists to use aggressive means in advancing their faith. State education is the most troubling illustration, in which secularism has ensured that its creation account alone be taught. With the exception of four states at present, which have science standards that include learning about the scientific controversy around Darwin's theory, evangelism for this secular doctrine is a staple of tenth-grade biology class. And make no mistake, in the sense of presenting as dogma the answer to an ultimate question, biology students at public high schools are being taught theology.

The key point is whether, across hundreds of millions of years, the development of life was guided or not. On one side of this chasm between worldviews are Darwinists, whose belief system asserts that life, through a material mechanism, designed itself. On the other side are theories like intelligent design (ID), which argue that no such purely material mechanism could write the software in the cell, DNA, or create the "irreducibly complex" nanotechnology in living cells—both of which present telltale signs of having been designed by an intelligence outside nature, as do other features of living systems and of the universe itself.

Both views, Darwin and design, have theological implications. The design view lends support to belief in a theistic deity, of any religious tradition or of none currently known, while Darwin radically undercuts such belief in favor of atheism. It really is that stark.

Darwinism would put God out of business. God's authority to command our behavior is based on His having created us. By this, I don't mean that He formed the first person from clay less than six thousand years ago, but that His guidance was necessary to produce the chief glory of the world, life. If the process that gave us existence was wholly blind and unguided, as Darwinism asserts (against the trend of scientific evidence, as a growing minority of scientists argue), then God is not our creator.

Yes, there have been some earnest but lame efforts to reconcile God and Darwin. You will hear people say, "Well, Darwinism doesn't mean God isn't the creator. Maybe evolution was programmed into the universe from the start. So He had no need to guide the process." The problem with such thinking is that it's directly contradicted by the major current in Darwinian evolutionary theory. In his book *Wonderful Life* (1989), the late Harvard paleontologist Stephen Jay Gould demonstrated what he called the "contingency" of life's history. Gould explained what an incredibly lucky break it was that earth ever cast up intelligent life-forms.

The science of Darwin's theory may be debated by reasonable and intelligent people, but not its clear theological implications. Yet debate is exactly what the biology curricula of almost every state and school district in the country will not allow. To increase the attention given to evolution in school science standards, by allowing teachers to present both sides in the Darwin debate, has been the case made by thoughtful intelligent design advocates. The secular theocrats reject it, preferring to teach Darwinian theory as unquestioned religious dogma.

A step forward would be to shatter the secular theocratic control of schools by allowing students to hear dissenting scientific views—not for biblical-literalist creationism, which has no serious scientific case, but for scientific critiques of Darwin. Really that is all that is required—simply to allow divergent views to be heard. Such debate is, for the biblical believer, not a compromise on the road to imposing *our* theology but instead the ideal prescription for great controversies like the one surrounding the question of evolution's mechanism. There is ample scriptural precedent for allowing conflicting opinions on ultimate questions to be aired openly and decided empirically.

In the period of the dual monarchies of Israel and Judah, the prophet Elijah challenged the false prophets of the god Baal. He asked their followers, "How long will you dance between opinion? If the Lord is the God, go after Him! And if the Baal, go after it!" (1 Kings 18:21). Elijah instructed the Baal party to join him on Mount Carmel and prepare a bull for sacrifice, while the prophet would do the same with his own bull. Then, "You shall call out in the name of your gods and I shall call out in the Name of the Lord, and whichever God responds with fire, He is the [true] God!" (18:24). Despite the best efforts of Baal's prophets, who danced and cried

out and cut themselves with swords, the pagan god failed to respond. But Elijah's God, despite the prophet's dumping jugs of water on his altar to retard the flames, dispatched a tongue of fire that
consumed the sacrifice and licked up the water. This had the desired
emotional impact on the people gathered on the mountaintop, who
prostrated themselves and called out to God in repentance.

Today, it's Christian and Jewish theists—some of them—who insist they can "dance" between the two opinions of Darwinian secularism and a viewpoint open to seeing a Deity's hand at work in the
universe. The Bible would favor allowing these rival worldviews to
battle it out, preparing arguments instead of bulls. One can say in
praise of Baal's prophets that, wrong though they were, at least they
had the courage to accept the challenge. By contrast, you have to
wonder about a theory like Darwinism, so brittle that its teaching
has to be mandated from above, compelling students to believe and
teachers, if they harbor doubts about Darwin, to be silent.

There is an element of totalitarianism in the secular theocracy as
it manifests itself in public education. Nor does it do so only in high
schools. Public universities and other government research organizations are implicated too (quite apart from private ones, which are no
better but at least make no pretense of being answerable to voters).
Scientists at these places who doubt Darwin are beleaguered. If they
don't have tenure, they are silenced, as indicated by cases at Ohio
State, Iowa State, and the Smithsonian Institution that I've covered
as a journalist.

But that is the way with intellectual totalitarianism. The Bible
and history together should have alerted us that in the very idea of
public schools there was potential for this abuse. That, I think, is
why the Jews for so long resisted establishing their school system,
for all their virtues. Not that we can go back to those better days.
But we can apply some of the insights that arise from the scriptural
ideal. In a biblical-constitutional democracy, the monopoly of the

secular theocracy would be broken, starting with biology class. It would be replaced with the free competition of ideas.

What should we say, then, about the question we began with, that of school prayer? Practically, it could only be contemplated if the intolerant secular theocracy's dominance were broken. Even then, the chief insight of the Bible on education is that when it comes to what matters most—giving kids an abiding sense of the reality of moral imperatives—that must come from the home, not the school. While education with its secular dogmas can reinforce cultural decay, the burden of generating moral authority falls primarily not on teachers but on parents. To expect public school teachers alone to halt the decline in traditional morals, by telling kids to "Just say no!" to sex or drugs, is too much to expect. Similarly, school prayer by itself, kids repeating a bland formula for half a minute each morning, will alone do little for their moral formation.

Secularists may fear the return of school prayer or teacher-led Bible readings. However, my own reading of the Bible suggests that to the institution of such reforms at this moment, God Himself—if we picture Him first as a Supreme Court justice casting the deciding vote and then as a persuasive member of the local school board—would be indifferent. Such reforms would be of importance only in the sense of being indicators that the culture of adulthood had regained some self-respect, the feeling it once had of authority to impart moral truths. In the absence of a revived parenting ethos, voting for or against prayer in school would be fairly meaningless. That is why the Bible lays such emphasis on the role of fathers and mothers, and none at all on the role of school.

II

⬦

SOCIETY

⬦

8

Poverty:
Getting Personal

We turn now from family issues to those with a public and national focus, beginning with a reminder of something I said
earlier. On the Left, there is no uniform discomfort with theocracy.
In a remarkable televised discussion by Democratic presidential candidates, the "Forum on Faith, Values, and Poverty" held in June
2007, left-wing activist Rev. Jim Wallis joined CNN's Soledad
O'Brien in posing a question to John Edwards. Wallis spoke of the
"gospel issue," the "biblical priority," of cutting the number of poor
in half in ten years' time. "As President," Wallis asked, "how would
you mobilize the nation and take concrete steps to accomplish this
goal?" He wasn't talking about private charity, but about using the
government's coercive and taxing powers, and so was Edwards when
he heartily agreed with Wallis, declaring that his own policy agenda

would end poverty in thirty years. Republican candidates would never talk so boldly, which is one reason I'm writing this book.

When it comes to the state's obligations to the poor, Religious Left activists like Wallis and his Jewish counterpart, Rabbi Michael Lerner of *Tikkun* magazine, lean very much to a theocratic approach. The Democratic presidential candidates in the 2008 election primaries were all comfortable seeing faith as the foundation of their own devotion to the needs of the impoverished. This is only a defanged, domesticated version of "liberation theology," popular with Marxist Catholic priests in Latin America and inspired by Matthew 25:31–46. The passage appears to indicate that a person's salvation is determined exclusively by how he treats the poor, the sick, and the downtrodden.

At first blush, a casual Bible reader might assume that the tradition of liberal compassion—which is different from conservative compassion—has a solid scriptural basis. But the assumption is wrong.

In his best-selling book *God's Politics* (2005), Jim Wallis counts three thousand separate biblical references to addressing the plight of the poor. While many of these instances are of uncertain relevance (Amos's "Let justice roll down like waters, and righteous like an ever-flowing stream" or James's statement that "faith without works is dead"), it is nevertheless clear that the Bible wants us to care for the unfortunate. Wallis devotes especially lavish praise to an outfit called Bread for the World, "the Christian hunger organization, [which] does some of the best work on Capitol Hill, focusing the energy of faith communities on budget priorities for hungry people around the world."

None of Wallis's scriptural quotations shows clearly who God wants to be the party primarily responsible for that care. Wallis rightly argues that the good of the needy cannot be adequately ensured without state involvement, but he often seems to let individuals off the hook, casting the burden of the poor on the political commonwealth. Can it really be that God is most pleased when, instead of digging into our own pockets to help the needy, we use the power of taxation to force other people to dig into their pockets?

For Christians, the question is especially pointed, since, even more than the Hebrew prophets', Jesus's role as champion of the poor is celebrated by religious liberals. In his book *The Politics of Jesus: Rediscovering the True Revolutionary Nature of Jesus' Teachings and How They Have Been Corrupted* (2006), African Methodist Episcopal clergyman Obery M. Hendricks Jr. emphasizes the context of impoverishment surrounding Jesus's ministry. Palestine in the first century C.E. is made to sound suspiciously like America under the Bush administration as many leftists describe our country with "two classes, the very rich and the very poor," the former constituting "a tiny upper class, no more than 5 percent of the population," the latter being "poor, many to the point of destitution." Actually, the voluminous rabbinic teachings from about this time give little indication that the overwhelming majority of Palestinian Jews suffered such grievous deprivation.

But questions of historical interest may be put to one side. On this issue, what the approaches of modern liberal activists and politicians have in common is the exaggeration of poverty's impact, the misplaced reliance on government to solve the "problem," and finally a disingenuousness about the motivation behind the crusade for the "poor."

Let's first get clear the scope of poverty in America. In the summer of 2007, candidate John Edwards went on a ballyhooed eighteen-hundred-mile "poverty tour" (as cynics called it) of economically stricken communities in Ohio, Pennsylvania, Louisiana, and elsewhere. The exercise produced photographs of the perfectly coiffed Edwards looking compassionate. Edwards's campaign manager told reporters, "We think it's an important issue when 37 million Americans wake up every day not having enough to eat or worry about how they are going to clothe their children."

What a wild exaggeration that is. According to the U.S. Department of Agriculture, in 2002, 89 percent of the American poor reported that they had "enough food to eat" year-round. If we assume a figure of 37 million "poor" Americans total, that means about 4 million did not always know where their next meal was coming from. As for the bit about worrying how to clothe their kids, the U.S. Census Bureau reports that 70 percent of the poor have, by their own estimation, enough income to meet "all essential expenses." The 30 percent who can't pay their bills would add up not to 37 million but to 11 million. From personal experience, I have known what it means not to be able to pay all the bills. It's terrible. But there is no justification for pretending that 37 million of our fellow citizens are in that uncomfortable position when the true number is less than a third of that.

While there may be no condition more humiliating than to be really poor, the lifestyle of America's "poor" presents a much more comfortable profile than any biblical writer would have been familiar with, or even than the middle class today living in other countries knows, including First World countries like those in Europe. The average poor American has more housing space (438 square feet per person) than the average European regardless of wealth (396 square feet per person), as reported by the European Union in 2002. According to our federal government, based on the 2001 American Housing Survey and the 2001 Residential Energy Consumption Survey, 46 percent of the American poor own their own home, 76 percent have air-conditioning, 34 percent have a dishwasher, 73 percent have a car, 97 percent own a color TV, 55 percent have two or more color TVs, 78 percent own a VCR or DVD player, and 62 percent get cable or satellite TV.

It is debatable whether the Bible's many admonitions to care for the poor really apply today, in the United States, other than to a relatively small number of people.

✧

But for the sake of argument let's assume that Edwards and other Democratic candidates, like Barack Obama, were not being misleading in citing that figure of 37 million poor. The question before us is how, in a society driven by a biblical worldview, the needs of the impoverished should be addressed. Obama sees the key as lying in the hands of the government. As his campaign literature makes clear, only the government can fund "transitional jobs programs," "establish public-private partnerships to lift up low-wage workers," "strengthen the federal Jobs Access and Reverse Commute program," "strengthen Small Business Administration programs that provide capital to minority-owned businesses," "raise the minimum wage," "expand paid medical leave," "increase the maximum Pell Grant," "create an Affordable Housing Trust Fund," "provide universal health care," and so on.

This is all very unbiblical. The first thing a scriptural worldview would note is that, with apologies to John Edwards, poverty can never be eliminated. On this, the Jewish and Christian Scriptures are united. Questioned by Judas about why Lazarus's sister Mary used expensive ointment on Jesus's feet instead of selling it to give to the poor, Jesus answered, "The poor you always have with you, but you do not always have me" (John 12:8). He was echoing Deuteronomy 15:11, where Moses commands the nation to be generous: "For destitute people will not cease to exist in the land; therefore I command you, saying, 'You shall surely open your hand to your brother, to your poor, and to your destitute in the land.' " Charity is needed precisely because the poor are always with us.

What's fascinating about that verse from Deuteronomy is that in the very same chapter, only seven verses earlier, is a statement that says the exact reverse! "However there will be no destitute among you; rather, the Lord will surely bless you in the land that the Lord, your God, will give you as an inheritance, to possess it, only if you will hearken to the voice of the Lord, your God, to observe, to perform this entire commandment that I command you today" (15:4–5). Which is it? There will be poor, or there will not be?

Years ago, I heard my friend Rabbi Daniel Lapin explain this. The Bible is telling us something profound about human nature. As long as there are differences in the gifts people have and in their inclinations for putting those gifts to work, as long as people are unequal, there will be differences in levels of affluence. Such distinctions "will not cease to exist in the land." Even in a prosperous society like ours, those citizens whose neighbors are wealthier than they are will be tempted to feel "poor." However, God gives us a piece of advice, of almost universal application: resist that temptation. Unless you are Bill Gates, you very likely know people with more money than you have. This can feel very much like poverty. But do not consider yourself poor. "If you will hearken to the voice of the Lord," taking His counsel, then "there will be no destitute among you." Rabbi Lapin explains that your *feeling* rich is indispensable to society's welfare. Those who *feel* poor don't contribute to the general good. They feel justified in opting for a life of taking. That is why biblical tradition lays it down as a law that not only the rich and the middle class should give to charity—10 percent of net earnings, following the patriarch Abraham's example of tithing (Genesis 14:20). Even a humble person must tithe his small income, to teach him that he is not poor, that there are others with even less than he has. (See Maimonides's law code, the *Mishneh Torah,* Laws of Gifts to the Poor 7:5.) What a disservice liberals do in telling 37 million Americans that they are always and forever "poor." How dispiriting and discouraging, not to mention inaccurate.

What would the Bible really commend as the preferred course of action for aiding those in need? Recently a little controversy was kicked up in the Seattle suburb where my family and I live. We read in the local weekly paper that a tent city for the homeless was to be set up in a church parking lot. In the article, representatives of the city government explained preemptively that the church had every right to do this with its own property and so the rest of us had no grounds for complaint. In a subsequent edition of the paper, a letter to the editor appeared making a fine and very biblical point. Would it not be better, the writer asked, if instead of setting up the tent city, members of the church invited individual homeless people to live with them? That would be so personal, so loving. It would also provide these needy individuals with role models: functional, successful families, a setting they may never have experienced, perhaps accounting for the dysfunction in their own lives that resulted in their being homeless. Graciously, she did not mention that this would not force an unwanted cost on the families that live in the homes adjacent to the church parking lot, who may feel very ill at ease having an encampment of transients as neighbors. Instead, the cost would be borne by the church's members who had made the decision to be generous.

I was proud that the letter writer, the lone voice of protest, was a Jewish woman. For this personal approach is exactly what the Bible commends to us. I can find nowhere in Scripture where the state is commanded to extend generosity to the impoverished. While society is indeed obliged, it is understood that the society is composed of *individuals,* bearing *individual* moral responsibility. It is, as ever, the mentality of *tumah* that tells us that individuals are incapable of being relied upon to meet this responsibility.

But is the letter writer's solution of private hospitality a remotely practical one? For some homeless, no. For others, yes. Who are the homeless, exactly? It depends on what part of the country you're talking about.

A 2005 head count of the homeless in Los Angeles County, conducted by the Los Angeles Homeless Services Authority, found that 24 percent cited unemployment as the main reason for their being reduced to vagrancy. The second largest group, 21 percent, said substance abuse drove them to the condition. Another 11 percent said it was a fight with a friend or family member, while 7 percent cited mental illness.

It's the able-bodied homeless that interest me. With many, neither illness nor addiction seriously bedevils them, but rather the culture of socialism that makes it possible to live a homeless lifestyle rather than seeking help from family and friends. The same culture excuses those family members and friends from getting involved. Private help on the biblical model doesn't seem to be an adequate response only because a liberal political environment has hypnotized us into thinking the government alone, or charity backed up by government coercion, can provide for the needy.

The Bible's first model of a responsible person, taking the welfare of the poor on himself, is Abraham. In Genesis, we observe him sitting outside his tent, recovering from having circumcised himself, when angels appear at the entrance of his tent in the guise of poor Arab wanderers. The tent was pitched in the desert, where no food or water could be obtained other than through hospitality. It happened that just then, Abraham was engaged in a conversation with God, an experience of prophecy. But he asked God to wait while, despite the pain of his physical condition, he ran to meet the wanderers and offer to prepare them a meal.

The book of Leviticus turns this ethos of charity into legislation: "If your brother becomes impoverished and his means falter in your proximity, you shall strengthen him—proselyte or resident—so that he can live with you" (25:35). Live with *you*, it says, not in the tent city that abuts other people's homes, nor in shelters funded by money taken by the government from other people. The prophet Isaiah was echoing the Pentateuch when he told the Jews living in his time, "Surely you should break your bread for the hungry, and bring the moaning poor [to your] home; when you see a naked person, clothe him and do not hide from your kin" (58:7). The emphasis on a personal relationship with the poor, not a pole's length interaction through the medium of government and taxation, is unmistakable.

⟡

Am I too hard on Democrats and other "progressives"? If their biblical interpretation is perhaps faulty, is their heart not in the right place? Isn't there something admirable, even if wrongheaded, in the socialist-tinged drive to deploy the state with its powers of coercion on behalf of the needy?

We need to grasp something about the underlying psychology of the Left. Every society and every person is given a radical choice. One can have faith in man and his ability to order society, relying on human wisdom alone. Among other problems with this option is the egotism in it, which shades over into tyranny. What justification does the man who is deemed less wise, less enlightened, have for insisting on his right to be free? He has none, which is one reason secular societies (like the old communist bloc) are so subject to totalitarian temptations. The other choice is to have faith in God, His wisdom, which can be relied on by all as we seek to design a just society. Because "God is not a man . . . nor a son of man" (Numbers 23:19), all humanity is rendered morally equal. None of us can pretend to be God. So no human, no matter how wise or enlightened, can claim a right to tyrannize other people.

The egotism inherent in secularism is what drives the socialist, and even the more moderate and prosaic figure of the American liberal, to think that if only his less enlightened fellow citizens gave him the chance to set up the laws just so, he could design the perfect society, eliminating poverty in thirty years.

The economist Thomas Sowell calls this secular delusion "the vision of the anointed," the temptation to see in politics mainly the opportunity to demonstrate your own superiority. Very appealing for liberals is the selection of "mascots." These mascots are other people, supposed victims of oppression—the poor, the homeless, minorities, gays—to whom are affixed "permanent labels." Liberalism's interest lies less in actually solving poverty or homelessness, than in manipulating the poor or the homeless in a kind of moralizing puppet show. That is why policy failures—like the 1960s War on Poverty, which actually ended up increasing welfare dependency—are shrugged off by liberals, rarely acknowledged as such. The results really aren't the point of the policy exercise. The real point is to allow the anointed elite to demonstrate their own wisdom and compassion, in contrast to the stupidity and selfishness of the benighted—usually, Republicans.

Thomas Sowell delineates this element of liberal psychology in his book *The Vision of the Anointed: Self-Congratulation as a Basis for Social Policy* (1995). But as ever, the Bible was there first. God commands, "Do not glorify a destitute person in his grievance" (Exodus 23:3). There are several reasons you might choose to "glorify" the poor. One is for the prestige reflected on you by your ostentatious display of compassion.

Another verse, cryptic but relevant, appears in the book of Proverbs: "Charity will uplift a people, but the kindness of nations is a sin" (14:34). Some translations give a different rendering that departs from the literal meaning and sounds like a platitude: "Righteousness exalteth a nation: but sin is a reproach to any people," as the King James Version puts it. But as the Hebrew original indicates, two kinds of charitable-seeming behavior are being described, one that has an authentically noble motivation, the other that proceeds from a questionable purpose. We would be at a loss to say more were it not for the earliest biblical interpretative traditions, transmitted by the rabbis in the Talmud. In tractate *Baba Batra* 10b, Rabbi Eliezer passes along to us the tradition that the proverb contrasts commendable charity with a preening, self-congratulatory so-called kindness done "only to magnify oneself."

Don't be fooled, in other words, by kind-sounding talk whose primary purpose is to solicit admiration or contribute to the self-esteem of the person doing the talking. God isn't interested in letting us use the poor to boost our own sense of personal prestige. He would favor candidates who refrain from making pious pronouncements about how they will end poverty in the historical blink of an eye, and who instead recognize that the kind of charity that truly uplifts is the private, not the government, kind. That's not to say the state should provide no safety net when individual generosity doesn't suffice. Yet in a biblical America, the emphasis should be decidedly on people helping others through their own free choice.

9

Taxes: In God's Image

Deciding how high taxes should be, unlike contemplating how to meet the needs of the poor, is an activity few of us automatically associate with feelings of spiritual uplift. Yet in a political culture informed by the biblical worldview, taxes would be considered a very spiritual topic, as even some liberal clerics would agree. A prominent Evangelical Christian pastor, Tony Campolo, complains in his book *Letters to a Young Evangelical* that "the folks currently in Washington do not have much of a heart for the poor." He includes as evidence the 2006 federal budget: "The new budget provides major tax benefits for the richest people in our society. That's wrong!" In other words, it's wrong to let people keep more of their own money than was previously the case.

Sorry, Rev. Campolo, you've got that backward. Cutting taxes, fighting the temptation to indulge in the redistribution of wealth, is the authentically biblical position. In his anti-Republican polemic *American Theocracy,* Kevin Phillips derides the " 'theology' of tax cutting as an item of faith, not logic." In fact, the Bible lends its authority to one side in a philosophical debate about what it means to be human, which in turn has implications for tax policy. You could take the same view the Bible does but for other, nonreligious reasons.

What does the Bible say? Over a millennium and a half of the history covered by the combined Jewish and Christian Scriptures, from Joseph to Jesus, there is a recurring motif on the theme of taxation. In Genesis, the patriarch Jacob's son Joseph becomes viceroy of Egypt. He gets the job because of some shrewd advice he had given Egypt's king, Pharaoh, about managing a coming seven-year food shortage by laying up a supply of reserve grain. When the famine hit, there was sufficient food to save the country from starvation. However, Joseph made the Egyptians sell themselves and their land to the king. "Joseph said to the people, 'Look—I have acquired you this day with your land for Pharaoh; here is seed for you—sow the land. At the ingathering of the harvests you will give a fifth to Pharaoh; the [other] four parts shall be yours—as seed for the field, and food for yourselves." In this way, the Egyptians agreed, "We will be serfs to Pharaoh" (Genesis 47:23–25).

Notice the equation of a 20 percent tax with serfdom. Notice too that currently (according to the Tax Foundation in Washington, D.C.) the average total tax burden, including federal, state, and local taxes, on an American taxpayer was 32.7 percent for 2007. In some states, the burden is significantly higher. In Connecticut, the highest taxed state in the country, it is 37.5 percent. In New York state, 36.5 percent. In California, 33 percent. One could make a solid biblically grounded argument that such a situation amounts to serfdom.

Centuries after Joseph's lifetime, the children of Israel settled in the holy land. At first, they were ruled by judges. Eventually they tired of this system and wished to be governed like any other people. They wanted a king. The people brought this demand to the leading figure of the day, the prophet Samuel. He was grieved by the request, among other reasons because the Jews failed to perceive that a king with his central government would mean high taxes. Samuel warned, "He will take a tenth of your grain and vines. . . . He will take a tenth of your sheep, and you will be his slaves. On that day you will cry out because of your king whom you have chosen from among yourselves—but the Lord will not answer you on that day" (1 Samuel 8:15–18).

That's right, a 10 percent tax amounts to slavery. Are we not slaves?

But the people of Israel refused to listen. A kingdom was set up over the land and it lasted through the reigns of Saul, David, and Solomon. The kingdom split in two, a disastrous event in biblical history, over the issue of excessively high taxes. What happened? It was after Solomon died, and his son Rehoboam ascended the throne, assuming the leadership of a restive people. The Jews appointed Jeroboam as their representative to the king, choosing this man perhaps because he had practical experience with the issue uppermost in their minds. Jeroboam had served under King Solomon as chief of taxation over the two tribes descended from Joseph's sons.

At the national assembly where the people elected Rehoboam as king, Jeroboam approached with a delegation of fellow Jews concerned about the tax burden left over from Solomon's reign. They declared, "Your father made our yoke [of taxation] difficult; now, you alleviate your father's difficult workload and his heavy yoke that he placed upon us, and we will serve you" (1 Kings 12:4).

Rehoboam, a foolish youth, first asked for counsel from the elders of the nation, who advised him to be conciliatory. But dissatisfied with the sound advice, the king asked his friends—young and callow like himself—what to do. They advised an aggressive stance.

Unfortunately, Rehoboam accepted their counsel. When the representatives of the people gathered to hear his response, he rebuked them: "My father made your yoke heavy, and I shall add to your yoke! My father chastised you with sticks; I shall chastise you with scorpions!" (12:14). In other words, far from cutting taxes, he would raise them. When the people heard this, the northern part of the country rebelled against the southern part, where Rehoboam still ruled. The northern kingdom, henceforth called Israel, split from the southern kingdom, Judah. The once-united Jewish nation was left divided and weakened. The kingdom of Israel survived less than 250 years. When Assyria attacked the north, its people were carried off into exile—the famous Ten Lost Tribes of Israel—never to be heard from again.

More than five centuries later, in the period of Roman domination of the land of Israel, the people were still sensitive about being overtaxed. At the time, the Jews were in political ferment, their anger at the Roman occupiers building to the point where it would boil over into the rebellion that resulted in the holy city's destruction by Rome in 70 C.E. As the first-century historian Josephus records, one of the four leading parties of the Jews was a group of radical anti-tax activists. In this context, Jesus was perceived as daring for even choosing to dine with tax collectors.

The foregoing narrative establishes how fiercely hostile to redistribution the political culture of the Bible is. Why is it that way?

Let's go further back in biblical history, to the creation of the first man with a soul breathed into him by God. Adam's receiving a soul from God is phrased in Genesis this way: "And God said, 'Let us make Man in Our image, after Our likeness. They shall rule over the fish of the sea, the birds of the sky, and over the animals, the whole earth, and every creeping thing that creeps upon the earth' " (1:26). The key points are: Anthropologically, man is unique among creatures in his being infused somehow with God's "image" and "likeness." And this giftedness has the consequence of man's being granted dominion over and responsibility for the rest of creation.

In our modern culture, the Bible's stance is increasingly controversial. The scholar Wesley J. Smith has written about the cultural struggle over the question of human exceptionalism. On one side, he notes, are the voices of those who deny that man is in any way distinct from nature, who affirm on the contrary that he is just an animal like all other animals, apart from being a little smarter. Those taking this view believe in "personhood theory," the bioethical doctrine that not only a human can qualify as a "person"—so can other beasts. They demand rights for animals along the lines of human rights. They affirm "deep ecology," which regards humans as a kind of vermin infesting the planet, endangering other species with our polluting ways. They deny the existence of a unique human soul— as in a recent *New York Times* science column by reporter Cornelia Dean, who concluded that evolutionary biology had proved that man has no soul, but rather that every emotional, spiritual, and intellectual faculty we possess can be accounted for materialistically as functions of the brain, just like with animals.

In biblical terms, this set of radical secular beliefs corresponds to the advice of the Serpent in the Garden of Eden, who sought to seduce Adam and Eve to join him on the side of the animals—to think of themselves not as unique creatures separate from the rest of nature, but merely as representatives of another animal species. The Serpent spoke from what Rabbi Samson Raphael Hirsch called "animal wisdom." Adam and Eve were, of course, led astray, with the result that God chose to expel them from Paradise to the world of suffering we live in now. The voice of animal wisdom is still confident and assertive today.

On the other side of this divide, opposing animal wisdom, are religious believers but others as well—agnostics who simply don't accept that believers in the people-are-animals doctrine have proven their case either philosophically or scientifically. The debate can be waged without reference to the Bible. However, for our purposes, it's clear that Scripture comes down on the side of human exceptionalism.

What does all this have to do with taxes? If people are unique, this has certain ramifications, with practical consequences.

One way that people partake of Godliness lies in our being, like God, creators. Even if you take the name of the Divinity out of the previous sentence, that is a sharp contrast to the worldview that competes with biblical religion in our society. Secularism follows the dismal eighteenth-century political economist Thomas Malthus, who portrayed life as a "struggle for existence," pitting animal against animal. In economics, Malthus's view leads to the gloomy belief that people are not creators but only consumers, competing with one another for scarce resources. Malthus's view languished in the middle of the nineteenth century until Charles Darwin made it the basis of his theory, a pillar of secularism. Darwin added that organisms maximized their chances of survival if they inherited favorable variations, later explained as genetic mutations.

In the Malthusian view, a person earns money not by creating value or wealth, but by taking it from other people. A wealthy man, then, is automatically suspect and must prove his virtue through charity or otherwise "giving back" to society.

This prejudice lies behind much of the outrage at America's wealthiest CEOs and their "obscene salaries"—in the phrase of Costco's chief executive James D. Sinegal. Robert L. Crandall, the former CEO of American Airlines, has, like James Sinegal, become a prominent critic of fellow business leaders. He complains that they "are the beneficiaries of a market system that rewards a few people in extraordinary ways and leaves others behind." Notice the language. A chief executive with a $1 billion net worth could only have achieved his riches by "benefiting from" the system—farming it, you might say. Did he benefit anyone? Apparently not. Like an unenlightened farmer, he continually depletes the soil until it has been thoroughly leached of nutrients. Crandall advocates "equalizing incomes" by imposing "much higher taxes than we have today."

Of course those with no experience heading up giant corporations are even more likely to resent rich rewards for company bosses. A July 2007 *Financial Times*/Harris poll showed that, when asked if such bosses should have their salaries capped, fewer than half of Americans said no. Admittedly, in the United States we remain less resentful than Europeans are. Asked the same question, two thirds of British and French respondents said yes, indeed, there should be a limit to wealth accumulation.

In such a value system, it seems fair and logical to redistribute wealth. But the Bible questions the underlying premise. As a creator on the model of the creator of Heaven and earth, man actually brings value into existence that hadn't been there before. God made the universe ex nihilo, from nothing. He didn't have to draw down other resources. Similarly, wealth is created, not merely taken. What better illustration could there be than America's richest individual, Bill Gates, whose software fortune adds up to 0.4 percent of the total national economy. Software is nothing more than data, coded information, that arose first in a human being's mind. The physical object on which the data is inscribed—your computer hard drive, let's say—is by itself of little value. But inscribed with coded ideas expressed in a string of 0s and 1s, it is worth a great deal. The information in the software that forms Bill Gates's wealth is not a physical but a spiritual commodity.

Even when riches derive from more physical sources, it is almost always the creativity added to the object that makes it valuable. Shoes, furniture, a car—beauty and function in a design derive from the mind, or the soul, just as the design of the world derived from God's mind.

A consequence of man's creativity is the sacredness of ownership with which the Bible invests our property. This is again on the model of God the creator. One of the titles bestowed on Him in Scripture is "God, the Most High, Maker of heaven and earth" (Genesis 14:19). The word translated as "Maker" (*koneh*) also means "Owner." To make something means to own it. Because God made the world, He is its absolute owner.

With humans too, the Bible takes ownership very seriously. The Pentateuch devotes abundant attention to laws having to do with property rights. You may not remove a marker indicating the boundaries of your neighbor's real estate holdings. You may not use dishonest weights, large and small, for weighing grain and other commodities—the Bible calls this an "abomination," the same word used to decry sexual perversions. If you find lost property, you are obliged to restore it to its owner. (See Deuteronomy 19:14, 25:13–16, 22:1.) And so on. The Tenth Commandment forbids us not from stealing but from coveting—that is, from so much as eying property that doesn't belong to you with a view toward extracting it from your unwilling neighbor's rightful ownership.

Biblical tradition can be surprisingly eloquent when reflecting on the nobility of ownership. Rabbi Daniel Lapin wrote an inspiring book on what many of us would, wrongly, consider a questionable topic for a man of God: *Thou Shall Prosper: Ten Commandments for Making Money* (2002). He argues that Jews have prospered economically the world over because they imbibed the Hebrew Scriptures' reverent attitude toward ownership and wealth.

The Hebrew Bible portrays money as a blessing to be sought. The central declaration of Jewish belief, the prayer *Shema*, emphasizes the material rewards that go to a society that "continually hearken[s] to [God's] commandments" (Deuteronomy 11:13). When Jewish parents bless their children each Sabbath evening with the text of Numbers 6:24–26, they have in mind the authoritative medieval commentator Rashi's explanation that one meaning of this priestly blessing is a promise of wealth: "May the Lord bless you and safeguard you." The meaning, Rashi says, is that God should bless your property and safeguard it from being taken from you. What's more, "The righteous value their wealth more than their own bodies" (*Chullin* 91a).

Which makes sense if money is simply the portable, exchangeable form taken by the Godly creativity you pour into your work.

Christian belief didn't immediately assimilate this Hebrew worldview. The New Testament displays a streak of ambivalence about wealth. One thinks of Jesus's famous teaching that "It is easier for a camel to go through the eye of a needle than for a rich man to enter the kingdom of God" (Matthew 19:24). The earliest church community, in Jerusalem under Peter's leadership, was fiercely communistic, insisting on the sharing of property on pain of supernatural death (Acts 5:1–11). There is a certain commonality of viewpoint with Greek philosophers like Aristotle, who, in his *Politics,* dismissed the life of the businessman as "ignoble and inimical to excellence." Later Christian thinkers, Augustine and Aquinas, denied absolute claims of ownership. Perhaps starting with the early Protestant theologians, Luther and Calvin, the Hebrew core of Christian teaching began to be recovered.

With all this in mind, we begin to see why the Bible is reluctant to endorse taking people's wealth from them. Scripture places the burden of justification not on the citizen who wishes to hold on to his money—for it represents the life force he has devoted to using his Godly powers to create—but on the government that would seize it. The government may tax people, but it had better do so with an attitude of reverence, awe, even fear, not entitlement.

There are two further consequences, relevant to taxation, of the radical divide between humans and animals.

First, equality of available resources is a condition associated rightly with animals, who we can all agree deserve to be fed and provided for (if they are domesticated) in proportion to their needs.

In a zoo, two lions of the same age, weight, and sex should be fed the same diet. There is no excuse for having a class of "rich" monkeys, zebras, or hippopotami. It would be fair to take all the excess hay from horses who had no need of it and redistribute it to other horses in need. But people—diverse in their creative gifts as in their personal inclinations as to how or indeed whether to use those gifts—are not animals. Diversity of economic conditions, variations of wealth and poverty, are to be expected. Equalizing incomes by taxation is a perversity. Rabbi Yosef Yitzhak Lifshitz makes this point in a brilliant essay, "Foundations of a Jewish Economic Theory," in the Israeli journal *Azure* (Autumn 2004).

As Lifshitz notes, biblical tradition finds no merit in equality, as can be seen from the scriptural legislation that forbids giving away all your assets. In his *Mishneh Torah,* Maimonides, the medieval codifier of God's law, explains Leviticus 27:28 in this way: A person who gives away all his money, becoming a beggar and a drain on society, is a "pious fool" and a "destroyer of the world" (Laws of Oaths and Vows 8:13).

Finally, to return to a central theme of my book, the distinction between people and animals expresses itself in the fact that people, unlike animals, bear responsibility for their actions. In this way too we partake of God's image. God acts freely, unconstrained by nature. People, when not infected with *tumah*-thinking, are aware of their freedom to make moral choices, which entails responsibility. A biblical society seeks to maximize this awareness that we can choose to do right or wrong, and that we should do right. When the government takes your money away and decides how it should be spent, implicitly the taxing authority has denied your freedom and your responsibility. No wonder Jonathan Sacks, the British chief rabbi, has written that "the Hebrew Bible is an extended critique of what we would today call big government."

Big government is only possible in an environment of heavy taxation. The more you are taxed, the greater the indication that we are living a culture based not on biblical values but on those of the alternative religion of materialism and secularism. The biblical version of society is inclined toward freedom, while the secular version inclines toward making decisions for us—in other words, toward tyranny. God would vote for freedom, which would necessarily entail reducing the overall tax burden to reasonable levels, certainly below 20 percent.

10

Race:
The Cost of Color Blindness

The dream of "race neutrality" or "color blindness" haunts our nation, a dream in which race fades from consciousness. "The country is poised to make a decision about race, about what its place in American life is going to be." So declares Ward Connerly, the businessman-activist who has organized a series of state ballot initiatives intended to block affirmative action in public education, employment, and contracting. He has had notable successes in California and Michigan. Connerly, a politically conservative African African, holds a view widely shared by many Americans. But not by the Bible.

Which may seem surprising. In the last chapter, we saw again that a biblically correct America would be a small-government sort of affair. Yet laws that spring from an awareness of race—affirmative action, for example—are more often associated with big government than with small. Well then, so be it. What I seek in this book is the politics of the Bible, not the politics of the Republican Party dressed up in biblical garb. A scriptural worldview is conservative, which can mean libertarian, but not simplemindedly so.

The vision of color neutrality was articulated in the grandest, most poetic, and scripturally tinged language by Martin Luther King. Indeed, religious language has a habit of sneaking into many a discussion of race in America. In his 1997 book *Liberal Racism: How Fixating on Race Subverts the American Dream,* journalist Jim Sleeper—himself a liberal—concluded with a call for "redemption" through race blindness: "This country's redemption has not and will not come through making race the organizing principle of our polity and civic culture. Liberals must lead struggles against discrimination and abuse. But for those struggles to succeed, in all endeavors liberals must let race go."

While King, Connerly, and Sleeper may appeal to our personal sentiments, a fair reading of the Bible suggests that "letting race go" is not at all what Scripture would recommend, neither at a practical nor at a philosophical level.

Practically, the Hebrew Bible provides a model of racially or ethnically based payback for previously experienced oppression. Blacks who call for affirmative action do so on the basis of wrongs committed against their enslaved ancestors. The ancient Hebrews would have appreciated such a demand for justice, even extending down through many generations. There is a strong biblical case that could be made not only for affirmative action but for reparations to African Americans, even if they are not currently suffering racial oppression.

Jews trace their origins to Israelite slaves in Egypt. When Moses led his people out of Egypt, he instructed them to request "from Egyptians silver vessels, gold vessels, and garments. The Lord gave the people favor in the eyes of the Egyptians and they granted their request—so they emptied Egypt" (Exodus 12:35–36). It was partial payment for 116 years of forced labor.

But those Egyptians personally owned Jews. No living American ever owned an African, and few have ancestors who did. What about Americans who are children of immigrants, who never participated in slave-owning? Aren't reparations fundamentally unfair?

According to biblical tradition, responsibility can be inherited, even by immigrants or (what amounts to the same thing in biblical terms) converts. Years before the Jewish people went down to Egypt, the patriarch Jacob's son Joseph was kidnapped by his brothers and sold as a slave to an Ishmaelite caravan. Generations later, when ten great Jewish sages were martyred by Rome, God is said to have approved it as retribution for the long-ago crime of Joseph's kidnapping. The story of the sages' death is recounted each year in the Yom Kippur liturgy. Interestingly, the most famous of these martyrs, Rabbi Akiva, was the descendant of converts. Though his own forefathers played no role in what happened to Joseph, he nevertheless paid the price.

Jews continue to pay. Two biblically based Jewish practices recall Joseph's enslavement and allow even Jews today to enact a sort of reparation. The scriptural commandment to pay a "redemption" price of five shekels for a firstborn son (Exodus 13:11–15, Numbers 18:16), and another commandment to dispense as an "atonement" a symbolic yearly half-shekel to the Jerusalem Temple or to one's local synagogue (Exodus 30:11–16), are both understood by the Midrash as payments toward the debt all Jews incurred in the crime against Joseph (*Genesis Rabbah* 84:18).

But this is less interesting than the Bible's philosophical view of race. To "let race go" would, in this perspective, be a great tragedy.

While the New Testament may be a different matter, the Hebrew Bible is very much concerned with racial identity, seeing in it a key aspect of God's plan for humanity.

There may be three or seventy such races in all, depending on what passages in Genesis you are looking at. Three great races of mankind are descended from Noah's three sons, Shem, Ham, and Japheth. After the Flood that destroyed the biblical world, Noah's family were the only humans left alive. Consequently, they and their children were responsible for rebuilding and repopulating civilization.

According to tradition, Shem became the ancestor of the peoples of Asia (including the Middle East). This is why Jews are called "Semites," meaning "Shem-ites." Ham fathered the peoples of Africa. Japheth, those of Europe. When you consider that the native inhabitants of North and South America came from Asia, whether by a land bridge from Siberia or across the Pacific, as did the aboriginal inhabitants of Australia, the Bible's threefold racial division would seem to cover all of humanity.

But Scripture offers, as well, a more detailed breakdown of the world's inhabitants. From Shem, Ham, and Japheth there descended a total of seventy primordial national units, listed in Genesis 10. We are told, "These are the families of Noah's descendants, according to their generations, by their nations; and from these the nations were separated on the earth after the Flood" (10:32).

Immediately following, we find the story of the Tower of Babel, whose point appears to be that God favors keeping national groups distinct. The people of Babel were engaged in constructing a forerunner of today's European Union, forcing once separate peoples into an amalgam, intended to erase national borders and ethnic distinctions. (Interestingly, the European Parliament building in Strasbourg, France, was designed to visually recall Pieter Brueghel's famous painting of the Tower of Babel.)

Babel's citizens wished to be forever united as "one people" (11:6), speaking "one language" and holding "one opinion" (11:1). When they built their famous tower, symbolizing this unity, the Lord responded by firmly fixing each nation as a linguistic unit, speaking its own language so as to be unintelligible to the people of any other nation. He then scattered them across the "face of the whole earth" (11:9).

Unique national identities are part of the divine plan for humanity. Can we say the same of races? Apparently so. One of those nations, Canaan, is descended from Noah's son Ham. Ham did something very inappropriate to his father that profoundly impacted Canaan's future. What exactly that was is unclear. However, it is hinted at obliquely. After the Flood, after Noah had established his little colony of survivors on the newly dried earth somewhere in the vicinity of Mount Ararat, the old man of the Ark planted a grape vineyard. He made wine, got drunk, and passed out cold.

"Ham, the father of Canaan, saw his father's nakedness and told his two brothers outside." A tradition in the Talmud suggests that, as the older man slept, Ham had homosexual relations with his father. As a result, God sentenced Canaan, Ham's son, to serve Ham's brother ever after: "Cursed is Canaan; a slave of slaves shall he be to his brothers" (Genesis 9:22, 25). It was Canaan's relationship to his father, the founder of the race of Ham, that determined his unhappy fate.

My purpose in relating these scriptural narratives is not to insist on it all as a literal rendition of history or to suggest that anyone should go out today and reenslave Canaanites. In any event, there are no Canaanites around anymore. Instead, the Bible is teaching us a basic principle. Despite the fact that the seventy primordial nations have been lost in the mists of history, nevertheless those national and racial identities that do exist count for something important. That could be negative or positive. Just as Canaan's relationship to Ham implied something negative about Canaan's destiny, a nation or a race can have a positive role to play as well. God gave unique missions to different ethnically related groups of people.

The Bible very clearly teaches this, to the point of obsession, about Israel. There is such a thing as a Jewish people, with an eternal mission, a message for the world about the relationship between morality and monotheism. But not only the Jews were given a unique role. The idea that there might be an African or African American approach to spirituality is not improbable at all. Is it "racist," in the sense of implying racial superiority? No more than the Hebrew Bible, in assigning Jews their unique role, is racist or ethnocentric.

Rabbi Elijah Benamozegh, a nineteenth-century Italian mystic, explained, "Each people has its own special character and embodies a particular idea, and so has an appropriate field of activity in which its genius must develop and express itself." He found this concept alluded to in Deuteronomy (32:8): "When the Most High gave nations their homes and set the divisions of man, He fixed the boundaries of peoples." On this verse, the medieval commentator Rashi explains, "When God divided the earth among the peoples, He gave every nation specific boundaries, so that each people might retain its particular identity." If you don't see how particular national identities implies particular spiritual missions, consider the alternatives.

There are basically two ways of looking at the world. There is materialism and there is spirituality. Materialism, in a philosophical sense, means the understanding of reality as being determined entirely by material, physical processes. Spirituality acknowledges the possibility that spiritual—nonmaterial and nonphysical—processes also play a role in shaping our world, maybe the dominant role.

In a materialistic worldview, the only way to account for the existence of different races is to point to a material process, evolution. In the Darwinian view, different races evolved not because a spiritual force, a designer outside nature, shaped them with a purpose in mind but because nature itself did so without a purpose.

This may sound like an inoffensive view, except that it has led to invidious comparisons between the races. Darwin wrote his book about human origins, *The Descent of Man* (1871), in part to explain the existence of different races, especially the ones he regarded as inferior or "savage." He reflected in passing, "At some future period, not very distant as measured by centuries, the civilized races of man will almost certainly exterminate, and replace, the savage races throughout the world." A horrific thought, but not a surprising one if you assume, as Darwin did, that no race has a divinely given purpose in existing.

The alternative worldview, spirituality, is by contrast well suited to entertaining the possibility of nations, peoples, and races having just such a purpose. Because the race issue in America is predominantly about blacks, not Jews, let's conclude by asking what blacks have to teach the world. What is their contribution?

I've heard a South African rabbi, David Lapin, lecture on this. He cited a story, recorded in the midrashic work *Tanchuma,* as a meditation on a verse in Psalms: "You save both man and beasts, O Lord" (36:7). The story tells of an African king who had the opportunity to rebuke Alexander the Great. Alexander visited an African kingdom to observe how its system of justice worked. In Alexander's presence, the African king was presented with a case of two men who had a disagreement about a treasure. One man had sold the other a ruined building in which, later, the purchaser discovered a buried treasure.

But these men were highly ethical and each feared to take the treasure from its rightful owner. The seller of the ruin thought the other man should take it. The purchaser thought, since he didn't realize he was buying a treasure but merely a ruin, the seller should take it. The African king came up with a brilliant and beautiful solution. One of the disputants had a son, the other a daughter. The son and the daughter should marry. They would then jointly inherit the treasure.

When Alexander commented that, in his own country of Macedon, the king would be entitled to execute both disputants and take the treasure for himself, the African monarch replied that he was surprised that God did not curse Macedon with darkness and drought for its wicked ways. He concluded it must be for the sake of the animals in the country that He was merciful. The Midrash goes on to note that this is one way of understanding the verse in Psalms: "You save both man and beasts, O Lord." The verse could also mean, in certain unethical cultures, "You save man because of the merit of beasts, O Lord."

As Rabbi Lapin observed, the Midrash may be telling us something about the special wisdom of Africans. In the story, the African king solves an ethical dilemma by appealing to the power of human relationships. Lapin pointed out that in the Bantu language of South Africa, there is a word for this idea: *ubuntu*. Desmond Tutu and Nelson Mandela have both spoken eloquently about it as a principle they hope will inspire the new South Africa.

Basically, *ubuntu* means not feeling diminished by another person's enrichment. When one person benefits, that's something to rejoice in, not to resent. This virtue is the opposite of coveting. Our country could do with a touch of *ubuntu*.

I don't mean that African Americans are necessarily infused with that virtue. But the Bible is holding out to us a vision in which we can assume (or hope) that every ethnic group has a unique cultural contribution to make, without which the rest of us are poorer.

Part of the rationale for affirmative action, and "diversity" programs, is to render a sort of payback for historical injustices. Another part, and a more important one, has in mind the good of the culture as a whole. There is a value in seeking to ensure that major

institutions—schools, colleges, businesses—include a broad representation of ethnic groups, rather than allowing representation to be
based strictly on merit and other factors having nothing to do with
race.

Letting race go from our consciousness may seem attractive. Indeed,
it has to be admitted that, on this issue, the Jewish and Christian
renditions of Scripture differ. All the passages I have alluded to so
far in this chapter come from the Hebrew Bible. The New Testament
appears to dismiss Jewish Scripture's insistence on separate peoplehood. St. Paul envisioned a race-neutral world, free of many of the
distinctions we take for granted: "There is neither Jew nor Greek,
there is neither slave nor free, there is neither male nor female; for
you are all one in Christ Jesus. And if you are Christ's then you are
Abraham's offspring, heirs according to promise" (Galatians
3:28–29).

It makes sense that the Hebrew Bible would emphasize national
identity while the Christian Scriptures do not. The Hebrew Bible's
great theme is to describe the mission of one particular nation, the
Jews, a "kingdom of priests" (Exodus 19:6), called to minister to
and teach others about God. In the Christian reading of sacred history, the Jewish mission has already been accomplished in giving the
world Jesus Christ, their most famous native son. So nationhood
may be discarded as a relic of a previous historical period. In the
Jewish view, that of the Hebrew Bible, the Jewish mission is as vital
as ever. It was never obviated by the ministry of Jesus. So the importance of particular national identity persists.

To "let go of race" would entail letting go of the possibility that
each race, each people, has a unique spiritual contribution to make,
which it can only do if it retains a distinctive and separate identity.
That would not, I think, be the preference of the God of Israel. If
He, let us imagine, lived in a state where Ward Connerly had put up

a ballot measure forbidding government affirmative action, He would break His generally right-leaning pattern and vote against it. If we follow the logic of the Bible, it seems thinkable that He could depart even further from standard conservative doctrine and at least not rule out the idea of paying reparations to African Americans.

11

Health Care:
The Purell Constituency

Amerian culture is suffused with fears of illness. In this hypochondriacal environment, the intensive politicization of health care was inevitable. More surprising is the way political liberals have sought to give a religious cast to their views on the issue.

At the June 2007 "Forum on Faith, Values, and Poverty" for Democratic candidates, it was as a preamble to touting her ambition to provide medical insurance for 45 million uninsured Americans that Hillary Clinton made the striking comment that I quoted in Chapter 1: "I think you can sense how we are attempting to try to inject faith into policy." Rev. Jim Wallis writes in his tub-thumping Religious Left manifesto *God's Politics,* "Rather than suggesting that we not talk about God, Democrats should be arguing—on moral and even religious grounds—that all Americans should have economic

security, health care, educational opportunity and that true faith results in a compassionate concern for those on the margins."

Whether the affordability of medical insurance could be im-
proved by market or mandate strategies is the highly partisan form
the current political debate has taken, a debate in which the Bible
would very clearly come down on the market side. Take a deep
breath, religious conservatives. After our detour of the last chapter
into the potentially statist aspects of our biblical democracy, we're
back on the small-government track.

What would the prophets say about our contemporary situation
where you can hardly turn on a TV or gaze at the cover of a
newsweekly magazine without being hectored about some disease
or condition? A bottle of the antiseptic Purell has become a contemporary icon, ubiquitous in offices, cars, and purses.

Everyone seems to agree that the accessibility of quality medical
care isn't what it should be, with "only" 84.3 percent of the public
having health insurance, according to Census Bureau data. Speaking
to what we might call the Purell Constituency, Hillary Clinton has
said, "We need a movement. We need people to make this the No. 1
voting issue in the '08 election." Michael Moore's film *Sicko* claimed
to document the egregious inadequacy of U.S. health care in comparison with the shining example of European nationalized medicine. For the staggering cost of care and of insurance, conservatives
blame out-of-control medical lawsuits. Conservative analysts call
for repairing the system through free market fixes, like providing a
standard tax deduction for those who buy insurance, and through
tort reform. Liberals prefer government mandates where the provision of insurance would be regulated, as in the current Medicare
system or along British, French, or Canadian lines.

In the most ambitious Democratic plans, every American would
be required to obtain insurance, or it would be provided for him.
When candidate Barack Obama offered a proposal stopping short
of this standard of truly "universal" health care, he was criticized by

liberals like *New York Times* columnist Paul Krugman. The journalist grumbled that "the Obama plan doesn't mandate insurance for adults," meaning that "some people would take their chances" and not buy insurance.

Mandating what seems to be common sense (making sure you have health coverage), and precluding the individual's freedom to take his chances if he prefers, places "universal health care" on the list of those other liberal political notions that foreclose free choice and moral responsibility. We saw earlier that John Edwards includes in his vision of universal coverage the requirement that Americans consult a doctor regularly. The Bible emphatically insists that adults be given responsibility. Market solutions to problems like our health care "crisis," whatever their other virtues, cast citizens as responsible individual moral actors. For that reason alone, the Bible would be opposed to most liberal schemes to fix health care.

True, you can point to verses that appear to criticize governments for not taking care of their citizens' health. The prophet Ezekiel castigated the rulers of Israel, her "shepherds," who failed to ensure the welfare of the people as a good shepherd tends his flock: "Woe to the shepherds of Israel who have tended themselves! Is it not the flock that the shepherds should tend?" Ezekiel lists among the failures of these rulers that "the frail you did not strengthen; the ill you did not cure; the broken you did not bind" (34:2, 4).

One question, then, is how best to assure access to quality medical care. Liberals are wrong when they minimize conservative doubts about following the model of Canada or the United Kingdom. In his 2007 book *Sick: The Untold Story of America's Health Care Crisis—and the People Who Pay the Price,* liberal journalist Jonathan Cohn mocks Republicans with their "wildly exaggerated" accounts of universal coverage and its shortcomings, accounts of "rationing and waiting lines, followed by a horror story from Britain or Canada." But there was nothing "wildly exaggerated" about the 2005 ruling by Canada's extremely liberal Supreme Court that Quebec could not constitutionally ban citizens from buying private insurance if, as is the case in Canada according to the country's highest court, "the public system fails to deliver reasonable services."

But aren't there circumstances where the government legitimately blocks choices we might make because they are inherently irresponsible? Is it ever legitimate—rational—for an individual to forgo medical insurance?

A growing percentage of the uninsured are those who make a decent living but feel they are young and healthy enough not to bother with health insurance. The number of uninsured poor is actually falling. (This is according to the National Center for Policy Analysis.) Writing on the Web site of the conservative magazine *National Review,* Iain Murray recalled his personal decision, during a lull in employment for a few months in 2003, not to buy insurance for himself or his wife: "I weighed the definite cost against the theoretical benefit and concluded that I could live with the risk." Murray was placing his interest in wealth over his interest in health, a trade-off whose wisdom the Bible endorses—or as the Talmud puts it, "The righteous value their wealth more than their own bodies" (*Chullin* 91a). I touched on that idea in the previous chapter.

But can it be right? Take a look at the book of Job. The sufferings of Job, visited upon that upright and innocent man in order to test his moral courage, included every sort of tragedy except one. Job lost his children, his livestock, and his health. He was a very wealthy person but, from a reading of the scriptural text, it doesn't appear that he lost his money. In the detailed account of his trials, there is no mention of his being deprived of gold or silver.

Most of the book of Job is taken up with the title character's discussions with his friends about the meaning of his suffering and of human trials in general. In Chapter 36, his friend Elihu gives a speech about the methodology of God's treatment of human beings. Much of the book is highly cryptic, so to understand what is being said, we have to rely on classical commentators who transmit ancient oral traditions explaining the otherwise hard-to-penetrate verses.

One of Elihu's statements is noteworthy: "Beware," he tells Job, "do not turn to iniquity, for you chose this over poverty" (36:21). As the medieval commentator Rashi explains, Job was tempted to wish another fate for himself, that God "should have judged me with the suffering of poverty," leaving him with his health, let's say, but without his wealth. Rashi goes on to explain, "These sufferings [of Job] are to be chosen above poverty."

Wouldn't a sensible person choose health over wealth? Not necessarily, as Rabbi David Lapin explains. It has to do with your attitude to life. Most of us see our relationship to the world as an exploitive one. We are put on earth to enjoy things and people. If you are sick, you can't enjoy anything including your money.

But that is not how the Bible wants us to conceive of our earthly mission, which is not to exploit but to create and contribute. Having that attitude turns many accustomed cultural values on their head. One is the presumed rational trade-off between health and wealth. A sick person can contribute and he can create, if he possesses the capital to do so. He can invest it and help build institutions from his hospital bed. A poor healthy person is far more limited in his ability to contribute to society on a wide scale.

For this reason, if we had to make such a choice, the Bible would have us choose wealth over health. It would be a shame if government policies, namely the imposition of universal health care, were implemented to make it impossible for a consumer to exercise such a risky but idealistic choice.

Scripture overturns many of our familiar assumptions. On the topic of health, we can go deeper, producing an even more startling insight. For the alleviation of sickness raises the question of what illness *means*. Why do people get sick?

The familiar medical answers focus on material causes—
unhealthy lifestyles, uncongenial microbes, unlucky genes. From
such a perspective, our culture's obsessive focus on confronting and
defeating disease and ill health makes sense. Why not devote the
government's vast power and authority to making sure everyone has
health coverage? Philosophically, materialism is the belief that physical reality is all there is. In this view, there could be no more pressing concern than to save your own personal health. While this seems
like a narrow, depressing, impoverished way of looking at life, on its
own terms it makes sense.

The Bible sees suffering differently. In a 2007 essay for the ecu-
menical journal *First Things,* Christian theologian Peter Leithart interpreted the prioritization of health care in the political arena as a
symptom of secularism. He cited another theologian, Edward Norman, who noted how Christianity "was founded in an act of expia-
tory pain"—Jesus's suffering on the cross, which in Christian belief
expiates sin—and how the Church therefore sees human suffering
likewise "as a necessary condition in spiritual formation." Spiritual
growth is achieved through pain, as Judaism would agree. By contrast, secularism cannot see how any positive purpose could ever be
served by suffering. It is only, again quoting Edward Norman, "an
affront or an impediment to the painless existence of men and
women."

There is strong evidence for this view in the Bible as a whole.
Plagues, various diseases, are a recurrent feature of the story of human history told by Scripture almost from the very beginning. But
in contrast to the modern secular worldview, sickness from God's
perspective is seen as possessing moral meaning. Almost always, it is
a wake-up call, a warning, a message to the individual or the community.

Take a few examples from the book of Numbers, which relates
the experiences of the Jews when they were living in the desert after
escaping Egyptian slavery. When Moses's sister Miriam spoke ill of

her brother's marriage, the Lord struck her with a mysterious skin affliction (*tzaraat*) that turned her flesh snowy white. She was healed only after Moses intervened with God on her behest.

Later, Moses sent spies to scout out the land of Canaan in preparation for the Israelites' entrance into it and the planned conquering of its inhabitants. When the spies brought back a discouraging report about the land and its supposedly fearsome natives, the Israelites broke out into hysterical fear of going up to fight the aboriginal Canaanites. God was so disgusted by this lack of faith on the part of the Jews that He proposed to "smite them with the plague and annihilate them" (14:12) until, again, Moses intervened.

Still later, when the Jews ungratefully complained about the poor refreshments being offered on the extended, forty-year camping trip in the desert, God sent poisonous serpents that bit "multitudes" until the people repented (21:6). Then the Lord had Moses fashion a copper serpent and suspend it on a pole. Those Jews who gazed upward on the serpent, and then cast their eyes to Heaven in faithful understanding that this plague came from God, were cured of the venom's deadly effect. It's ironic that the symbol of the snake on the pole later merged with a similar pagan symbol, the Staff of Aesculapius (a snake on a staff), as a symbol of the medical profession. In medicine, faith is not generally considered a tool of healing. In this biblical account, faith is the whole point.

In the Bible, God and His prophets are healers, while physicians are regarded with scorn. The point is conveyed in contrasting stories of two Jewish kings who became ill. King Solomon's great-grandson King Asa was one of the kingdom of Judah's virtuous monarchs but he died in a way that did him little credit. He had been on the throne for thirty-nine years when he was struck with an unnamed illness that began in his legs, spreading upward. Unfortunately, "in his illness he did not seek out the Lord, but only doctors" (2 Chronicles 16:12). This demonstrated his lack of faith.

Nine generations later, Asa's successor King Hezekiah became "deathly ill." The king did not consult doctors but instead prayed to God for healing (Isaiah 38:3). God responded favorably, adding fifteen years to his life.

Doctors treat only the superficial physiological signs of illness. Scripture's interest lies in the underlying spiritual reality. If a sickness is assumed to have significance, then the way to fight it is to address the moral condition that produced it, not merely to alleviate the symptoms as doctors do.

Maimonides, citing verses in the Bible (Numbers 10:9, Leviticus 26:27–28), argues in his *Mishneh Torah* that any plague must be regarded as a moral message. To ignore the message and treat it as the mere playing out of random natural forces is nothing less than "cruelty" because it deprives the community of the opportunity of reflecting on that message and amending their behavior as needed (Laws of Fasts 1:3).

The Talmud explains that in an ideal world, we would never consult doctors at all. A person with an illness would seek out spiritual guidance, not unlike the model of Christian Science. That we are allowed to use medicine is a leniency, a concession taking into account that few of us are up to the exalted spiritual level it would require to effect healing through repentance.

Does this mean that every time somebody gets sick, it's a punishment? No, of course not. First all, it is arguable from Scripture that intensive personalized providential direction—God's direct oversight of your every experience in life—is given only to very special individuals who choose the most intensive relationship with God (see 1 Samuel 2:9 with Maimonides's interpretation in the *Guide of the Perplexed* 3:18). Second, "punishment" is the wrong word anyway. Rather, God set the world up in such a way that moral reality interfaces with physical reality. There are rules of physics and chemistry, describing the interaction of physical objects. There are also spiritual rules, which describe how moral activity—actions whose significance is moral and spiritual—can produce physical results (like illness). It's not a punishment. It is how the world works.

Third, if you assume a more general divine providence, as I do, the meaning of an illness may imply nothing negative at all about the sick person. It may imply the opposite! Nor may that meaning be readily discernible. One of the Bible's most famous symbols of suffering is the Suffering Servant of Chapter 53 in the book of Isaiah, a person or personified group of people whose pain atones for or otherwise follows from the sins of others. Christians see Jesus alluded to in the prophecy, while Jews see a saving remnant of the Jewish people.

The pure and holy Suffering Servant will suffer severe illness: "He was despised and isolated from men, a man of pains and accustomed to illness. As one from whom we would hide our faces; he was despised, and we had no regard for him. But in truth, it was our ills that he bore, and our pains that he carried—but we had regarded him diseased, stricken by God, and afflicted!" (53:3–4). The Hebrew original, cast in the past tense, insistently uses language associated with literal, physical disease. Yet the "we," the population who regard the servant with contempt, mistakenly attribute his suffering to his own moral flaws. In fact, "the chastisement upon him was for our benefit" (53:5), reflecting our sins.

Though we shouldn't assume we know the meaning of an illness, we should assume it has one. The alternative is the meaningless, materialistic universe of secularism.

If materialism is the premise, then by all means, let us deploy the government to rid ourselves of our illnesses—of all illness, why not? As Barack Obama has said of imposing his own vision of almost universal health care, "It's the right thing to do."

In reality, illness is something to be treated with thoughtfulness, even—for the very mighty of spirit—gratitude. It would be much better to allow individual moral actors, responsible human beings in all their glory and pathos, to work out their own relationship to their illnesses with maximum freedom. This doesn't mean, obviously, that we should stop getting checkups with our primary care providers or neglect to have our ailments treated medically. Of course we must all act responsibly. Yet the Bible illuminates a theoretical model of how to relate to your health, a vision with definite public policy implications, radically at variance with the secular liberal one.

Will this latter vision of universal health care prevail? It is interesting to reflect that while almost all the developed world has turned to various models of government-directed medicine, America has resisted so far. That could be because our country, for all its weaknesses, remains the most Bible-believing in the world. God, unlike John Edwards, would vote to keep it that way, retaining the care of one's health as much as possible as an arena for free decision-making.

12

Capital Punishment:
Final Exit

Sometimes it seems that modern religion has been contrived to conceal and distort the plain meaning of the Bible. This is nowhere more blatant than on the issue of capital punishment. When the mass murderer Saddam Hussein was hanged in Baghdad in 2006, the Vatican's Renato Cardinal Martino, president of the Pontifical Council for Justice and Peace, protested that the American-sponsored Iraqi state was merely punishing "a crime with another crime." The latest Catholic Catechism feels that because the technology of modern, secure, humane imprisonment is available as an alternative, there is hardly a need at all for putting criminals to death. Thus, "given the means at the State's disposal to effectively repress crime by rendering inoffensive the one who has committed it, without depriving him definitively of the possibility of redeeming himself, cases of absolute necessity for suppression of the offender 'today . . . are very rare, if not practically non-existent.' " By "inoffensive," the Catholic text means, I assume, incapable of harming others.

In *God's Politics,* Religious Left guru Jim Wallis uses a clever formulation, writing of his belief in a "Consistent Ethic of Life," to link opposition to abortion with opposition to the death penalty.

I am not a fundamentalist, meaning someone who thinks the Bible can be read like a newspaper or high school textbook, always taking the apparent meaning (garnered from a translation, of course) as the true meaning. But every so often, the fundamentalist approach is the right one. Some themes in the Bible are so insistently sounded, and in such crystal-clear terms, that to dismiss the simple and straightforward interpretation becomes nearly impossible, if you are being honest with yourself. The acceptability of capital punishment is a good example.

Here, besides our resistance to government-directed health care, is another way America remains unique in the Western world—in practicing the death penalty while Europe sniffs at us in disapproval. Again, it has something to do with the fact that the United States is a society uniquely infused with scriptural values.

When the legal sections of Scripture describe its preferred methods for the enforcement of law and the punishment of lawbreakers, the need for executing notorious criminals is assumed everywhere. The Bible has four methods of execution: hanging, stoning, burning, and decapitation. The punishment is prescribed for a variety of sins, including murder but also many others that would properly apply only in a Jewish commonwealth. Because America isn't a Jewish commonwealth, we naturally don't penalize Sabbath-breaking.

But murder? "One who strikes a man, so that he dies, shall surely be put to death" (Exodus 21:12). That should be clear enough. Yet it's hard to find a respectable religion today that feels comfortable with the death penalty.

You expect no less from the liberal mainline Christian denominations, which have lost confidence in so many of the ancient doctrines they once stood for. So too the liberal Jewish denominations, which equally have been intimidated by modernity. About the same time the inaptly named Jewish Conservative movement was giving a green light to Jews to break the Sabbath by driving a car to synagogue, the movement's Committee on Jewish Law and Standards in 1960 rejected "all forms of capital punishment as barbaric and obsolete."

Even traditional denominations have buckled. The Union of Orthodox Jewish Congregations of America—the major traditional Jewish umbrella group—called in 2000 for a moratorium on executions until it could be determined that the death penalty claims only guilty lives, not innocent victims. Simultaneously, a legal clinic at the law school of the Orthodox Yeshiva University was tallying up the number of innocent men condemned to death and imprisonment as determined by new techniques of DNA analysis. As of May 2000, Y.U.'s Innocence Project had analyzed two hundred cases of DNA exoneration (since 1989). These included twenty-eight individuals wrongly convicted of murder, of whom fourteen were on death row at the time of their being pardoned.

As the work of the Innocence Project suggests, there are reasonable objections to the death penalty as it is carried out in the United States. But the Bible is well aware that human courts are human, prone to error. A special feature of scriptural jurisprudence is the falsifying of witnesses. A man may be convicted of a crime based on the testimony of two witnesses. But if two other witnesses then appear and testify that the first witnesses were somewhere else—not at the crime scene—when the supposed crime took place, then not only is the case dismissed but the original witnesses are subjected to the punishment that they, through false testimony, sought to inflict on the defendant.

The institution of witness falsification (Deuteronomy 19:16–21) assumes the possibility of a man's being falsely accused and falsely convicted. If a pair of witnesses who might have falsified the first pair get run over by a bus—or in a biblical setting, gored by a mad ox—on their way to the court, then it seems, tragically, that an innocent man will be executed. It would not occur often, but it could happen. To insist on a perfect system of justice, one that never makes mistakes, would be to utterly paralyze law enforcement.

Other objections, seemingly based on religious considerations, are less substantial. After briefly describing the penalty for murder as the Bible and traditional interpretations prescribe it, we will consider some of the more commonly heard religious cavils.

To carry out the penalty, certain strict conditions must be met. The condemned man must have been witnessed in his commission of the crime by two adult males of an unblemished moral character. Among other stipulations hammered out in much detail in the Talmud, the witnesses must see the crime being committed. They must warn the would-be criminal beforehand, informing him that he is about to commit a capital crime that will carry a penalty of such-and-such (hanging, stoning, burning, or decapitation). Later, they will have to stand up to the withering scrutiny of a Jewish court, empowered to trip them up with a complex series of questions meant to support or (more likely) undermine their testimony.

You will notice that biblical law has *no provision at all for punitive incarceration.* Contrary to the view implied in the Catholic Catechism, humane and secure imprisonment is no modern innovation. In Genesis, the Bible itself describes the experience of Joseph, son of the patriarch Jacob, who was imprisoned in Egypt on the false charge of sexually assaulting a married woman. We learn nothing about Joseph's having been mistreated in jail. It is not as if, then, the Bible were unacquainted with imprisonment. Instead, we have here a deliberate choice not to prescribe it as a punishment—a clearly expressed preference following from a definite theory of punitive treatment and its purpose. For murder, the penalty is imposed not to safeguard society, nor take revenge, nor satisfy a demand for blood, but out of the more mystical consideration that a human is made in God's image, and a blow to that image is also a blow against God. This is the Bible's clearly stated rationale for capital punishment, given unambiguously to Noah and his children upon their exiting the Ark to rebuild the world after the Deluge: "Whoever sheds the blood of man, by man shall his blood be shed; for in the image of God He made man" (Genesis 9:6).

The only case of a criminal being lawfully imprisoned, with Scripture's approval, occurs in the book of Numbers (15:32–36). Moses confines a Sabbath breaker just long enough to inquire of God what method of execution would be most appropriate. God answers, "The man shall be put to death; the entire assembly shall pelt him with stones outside of the camp."

Supposedly Bible-based objections to the death penalty face a steeply uphill climb against the gravitational pull of Scripture's manifest intent. These objections fall broadly into two categories. Some follow from an inappropriate focusing on some scriptural or other text or idea to the exclusion of other texts or ideas that would put the former in context. Others seem to follow from, as suggested earlier, a buckling to social and historical forces.

It will be helpful here to treat Jewish and Christian exegetic errors separately.

Jewish interpreters will make the seemingly reasonable point that if the biblical procedures for convicting a murderer (or a Sabbath breaker or an adulterer) were followed, it would be nearly impossible to convict anyone. Just consider the requirement of warning the criminal beforehand, not only that he is about to commit a capital offense but that if he does so he will suffer such and such a penalty. In the case of warning a Sabbath breaker, he also has to be warned which of thirty-nine categories of forbidden Sabbath labor, and which specific subcategory (if appropriate), he may be convicted of. If he is warned of the wrong category, this is grounds for dismissing the case against him. Even the Talmudic rabbis themselves could not always agree how a given Sabbath violation should be categorized. Pity the poor witnesses who had to make such a complex legal evaluation on the spot!

Executing someone for breaking the Sabbath was nearly impossible. The intention behind making breaking the Sabbath a capital crime in the first place, then, was not to create a society where violators are actually executed but rather to emphasize the seriousness of the matter.

Warning a would-be murderer presents problems of its own. Consider a crime of passion. In the time it takes the assailant to work himself into a fit of anger over, let's say, his wife's just discovered infidelity, will there really be an opportunity to fetch witnesses to warn him?

Jewish death penalty opponents argue that the sheer difficulty of imposing the punishment in the Jewish biblical commonwealth argues against those who see Scripture as positively proposing capital punishment to our own modern society. These Jewish thinkers point to Talmudic and rabbinic sayings that seem to bear them out. In the Talmud's tractate *Makkot* (7a), the rabbis declare a court to be "destructive" if it executes one convict in seven years. A stricter view says, even one in seventy years is too many. Rabbi Tarfon and Rabbi Akiva are then quoted as saying, "If we had been members of the Sanhedrin no man ever would have been put to death."

What critics of capital punishment rarely point out is that these famous statements are then followed immediately with the view of Rabbi Shimon ben Gamaliel, taken to be the authoritative view in the debate, that if the most restrictive view were followed and the death penalty effectively abolished, society would be awash in bloodshed by unpunished murderers.

Jews also like to quote a saying of the medieval sage Maimonides: "It is better and more satisfactory to acquit a thousand guilty persons than to put a single innocent one to death." That sweeping statement occurs in Maimonides's *Book of the Commandments,* Negative Commandment #290. The work lists the 613 commandments of the Bible. These same Jews invariably fail to quote the commandment that comes immediately before, #289, which directs that the death penalty be carried out where appropriate even if that means dragging the convicted man from before God's own holy altar. The scriptural proof text is Exodus 21:14.

How can we reconcile these seemingly contradictory impulses in biblical tradition?

The resolution is found in the unique biblical division of judicial functions into religious and secular branches. When it comes to punishing murder, the importance of the religious court, the Sanhedrin, seems mainly symbolic. But the Bible assigns the secular government, the king, a role too, that is deadly serious and not symbolic at all. In his digest of the law, the *Mishneh Torah* (Laws of Kings and Their Wars 3:10), Maimonides writes: "One who murders without clear proof, or without warning, even if [in the presence of] a single witness, or an enemy who kills unintentionally, the king has authority to execute him and to perfect the world in accordance with what the hour requires." King David availed himself of these provisions on at least two occasions (2 Samuel 1:15, 4:9), from which the parallel institution of the secular, royal prerogative is derived.

Perhaps the most important feature of the secular power to execute is that it need not be based on eyewitness testimony but instead may be based on circumstantial evidence, as in an American court. So Maimonides makes clear in his *Guide of the Perplexed* (3:40). Not that the matter is simple. For those who would like further information from an expert, Rabbi J. David Bleich has an excellent essay clarifying these issues, "Capital Punishment in the Noachide Code," published in his book *Contemporary Halakhic Problems,* Vol. II (1983).

For Christian critics of the death penalty, meanwhile, there is material to be drawn upon in the story of the adulteress taken out to be stoned, whom Jesus saves with the bold challenge to her would-be executioners, "Let him who is without sin among you be the first to throw a stone at her" (John 8:7). The incident is hard to accept as history, since it depicts "scribes and Pharisees" acting as a virtual lynch mob, when we have already seen how painstakingly hard it would be for the rabbis (aka Pharisees) to convict virtually anyone of such a crime. Nevertheless, from the perspective of Christian faith, you can see that the story poses a challenge to the imposition of a death penalty.

That is, if the incident really is told as a comment on capital punishment. It seems much more likely that it is a parable about judging others in social settings (not condemning your friends, co-workers, or family members for perceived faults), as opposed to the formal context of a courtroom. For elsewhere the New Testament is clear in endorsing the power of the state to act for justice, including taking a sword (for execution) in hand. In his letter to the Romans, the apostle Paul writes, "Let every person be subject to the governing authorities. For there is no authority except from God, and those that exist have been instituted by God. Therefore he who resists the authorities resists what God has appointed, and those who resist will incur judgment. For rulers are not a terror to good conduct, but to bad. Would you have no fear of him who is in authority? Then do what is good, and you will receive his approval, for he is God's servant for your good. *But if you do wrong, be afraid, for he does not bear the sword in vain;* he is the servant of God to execute his wrath on the wrongdoer" (13:1–4, emphasis added).

Paul was merely expanding on an idea found in the Hebrew Bible, that the state in some sense acts in the place of God, on His authority: "Like streams of water is the heart of a king in the hand of the Lord, wherever He wishes, so He directs it" (Proverbs 21:1).

✧

The real meaning of the Bible cannot be perceived except when surveying the book and its teachings as a whole. In light of the total scriptural context, verses that seem to be at variance with the Bible's great main themes can be reinterpreted, bringing them in line with Scripture as an organic totality. It should be clear that whether for a Jew or a Christian, the obvious way of reading the Bible on capital punishment is also the authentic way. How then can we understand the reluctance on the part of religious authorities to see this?

There are two ways of putting this reluctance in a social and historical context. Supreme Court Justice Antonin Scalia, a Catholic and a death penalty proponent, has spoken against his own church's stance in the matter, which *"everyone knows does not represent the traditional Christian view"* (emphasis in the original). It is interesting that the Catholic Church has felt obliged to depart from the "traditional view" while American Evangelical Christians—those lone holdouts—have not felt obliged. When Saddam Hussein was executed, Richard Land, the thoughtful president of the Southern Baptist Ethics and Religious Liberty Commission, had doubts only about the disorderly atmosphere surrounding the event, captured on video. Otherwise, commented Land, "Simple justice demanded Saddam Hussein be found guilty by his countrymen and executed in the manner that befits such a war criminal, by hanging rather than firing squad."

Why did the Catholic Church buckle? One possibility is the Church has a troubled conscience. When Catholic authorities had the power to takes lives, as in the Middle Ages and even after, they often abused that authority and so now the Church recoils from it. Understandably so. The Protestant Reformation, and modernity, swept political power from the Catholic Church. Today, Pope Benedict XVI studiously condemns any hint of the conjoining of spiritual with political authority. In his book *Jesus of Nazareth* (2007), Benedict writes, "The struggle for the freedom of the Church, the struggle to avoid identifying Jesus' Kingdom with any political structure, is one that has to be fought century after century. For the fusion of faith and political power always comes at a price: faith becomes the servant of power and must bend to its criteria."

By contrast, American Evangelicals have nothing like the Catholic Church's difficult history to feel pained about. There is no horrendous past of burning people at the stake. On the contrary, the special Protestantism associated with America has been consistently a friend of liberty. It can afford to affirm the traditional view without pangs of guilt.

On the Jewish side, there is probably a big admixture of the influence of modernity, the same influence that has sapped liberal Protestantism of its old confidence in tradition. In the Jewish community, one notes a will to appear genteel, which means imitating Episcopalians, an impulse driven by the social anxiety associated with being a recent immigrant. Alas, it is an old Jewish story.

For Jews and Christians alike, finally, the modern infatuation with materialism plays a role. Ever since Darwin sought to explain human beings as creatures not of a designing deity but of impersonal forces (random variation, natural selection), modern culture has been tempted to see people as passive objects in the grip of material powers of nature. Is a person morally responsible? Is he morally free to do right or wrong? On these two questions, materialism throws us into doubt.

In criminal law it has done so for more than eighty years. Clarence Darrow defended the notorious Nathan Leopold and Richard Loeb for their 1924 murder of a fourteen-year-old boy, Bobby Franks, in Chicago. His legal defense was novel at the time but has since become common sense for many liberal Americans. He decried the "old theory" that "a man does something . . . because he willfully, purposely, maliciously and with a malignant heart sees fit to do it." To this, he contrasted the new theory that "every human being is the product of endless heredity back of him and the infinite environment around him."

Today we would say, instead of heredity, DNA. From this it follows, if the criminal is not morally responsible, then neither are we who would execute him. He can't be held responsible. We can't take responsibility for such a final act. To hold him responsible would mean to put him to death. To hold ourselves responsible means to give ourselves the responsibility of making the decision to put him to death. The denial of moral freedom makes either possibility untenable.

Against such modern despair stands the faith of the Bible, with its insistence that men and women are free and responsible, sometimes, very sadly, with deadly consequences. In America today, we can take some pleasure in reporting, only twelve states plus the District of Columbia forbid capital punishment, including Michigan, which has had its legal ban in place for more than a century and a half, since 1847. If God lived in any of those states, He would vote to change the law.

13

Gun Control:
Armed and Dangerous

In the 2008 election, Rudy Giuliani has stood out from the pack of fellow Republican contenders with some seemingly liberal views. As New York's mayor, he was for abortion rights, for gay rights, and for gun control. He supported the Brady Bill (1993) and the federal assault weapons ban (1994). I've already suggested that the abortion issue should be considered a litmus test for biblically inclined voters. Yet on guns, there is not only room for debate, there is actually an argument for apparent heresy—a biblical argument for limiting access to weapons.

Whatever the Second Amendment to the U.S. Constitution means in affirming the right to bear arms as part of a "well regulated militia," the Bible on the surface certainly appears to take such a right for granted. The heroes of Scripture were nothing if not well armed.

Isn't it obvious that a biblical America would disdain the practice of gun control? On the surface, yes. But if you look a little deeper, perhaps not. It emerges that what we learned in the last chapter about the death penalty and its lesson about societal responsibility doesn't fully apply here.

The theme of weaponry appears early on in Genesis. When Lot, nephew of the patriarch Abraham (then called Abram), was kidnapped by invading armies from Mesopotamia, Abram took action. "And when Abram heard that his kinsman was taken captive, he armed his disciples who had been born in his house—three hundred and eighteen—and he pursued them as far as Dan" (14:14), in the north of the land of Israel. There, Abram organized a lightning strike on the Mesopotamian marauders from whom he freed Lot.

Abraham's descendants, the people Israel, were enslaved in Egypt but God freed them with signs and wonders delivered as blows against the Egyptian people. The Jews headed north into the desert wastes, making toward Israel, having taken precautions not to go unprepared for adventure: "So God turned the people toward the way of the Wilderness to the Sea of Reeds. The Children of Israel were armed when they went up from the land of Egypt" (Exodus 13:18). Presumably, like all the rest of the liberated Hebrews, Moses carried a sword.

Remember, these are figures—Abraham and Moses—not otherwise known as soldiers or generals. Of the latter, the Bible has many examples, starting with Moses's subordinate Joshua who led the Jewish invasion of the holy land against its then inhabitants, the Canaanites. The book of Joshua is a famously militaristic book. The deeds of such a military personality would, of course, prove nothing. No one would expect a soldier to go about unarmed. The point here is that even a civilian would be expected to possess armaments.

The Torah (Exodus 22:1–2), indeed, makes it a point of divine law that a private person has a qualified right to defend his home by violence, though the text doesn't state by what means the citizen is entitled to do so. The case given involves a thief who is discovered sneaking into your house. If the circumstances are such that his own violent intentions are a possibility, you may kill him. If you know he wouldn't hurt you, you may not kill him. Translated into twenty-first-century terms, we would have to ask how a householder would take such decisive action against a possibly dangerous burglar if the former had no weapon in his home.

Advancing in history to the era of Jesus, we find the Jews still far from a nation of pacifists. According to the first-century historian Josephus, when Jews gathered three times a year for the biblically commanded pilgrimage festivals (Passover, Shavuot, and Sukkot), they all went up to Jerusalem armed to the teeth. That is one reason the Romans' imperial legions, then in control of Palestine, found it so difficult to keep the restive Jews in a state of law and order.

On the occasion of a particularly momentous Passover, Jesus's own followers were armed, as is evident from the Gospels' story of the event at Gethsemane. Jesus took his disciples to the garden there, at the foot of the Mount of Olives, by night. When the betrayer, Judas, showed up with a "great crowd with swords and clubs, from the chief priest and the elders of the people," one of Jesus's followers drew his own sword and struck the high priest's slave, cutting off his ear. For this, Jesus reprimanded him: "Put your sword back into its place for all who take the sword will perish by the sword" (Matthew 26:52).

But isn't all this just a function of the time and place in which the Bible stories occurred? Maybe. Palestine was a pretty rough-and-tumble sort of a country. Our own modern American context, however scary at times, doesn't really compare. Weapons were different then too. You can't commit a "massacre" by sword, certainly not if you are a lone swordsman, with the same ease a gunman with a semiautomatic can mow down innocents. Surely this militates in the direction of considering the application of tighter controls on guns than on swords.

Then again, as Jesus's remark demonstrates, there is no denying that the Bible takes a complex view of weapons. Perhaps the most dramatic statement in that vein is God's own instruction to the Jews, delivered at Mount Sinai right after the Ten Commandments were given, not to build the holy Altar of the Temple in such a way that it would remind anyone of weaponry: "An Altar of earth you shall make for Me. And you shall slaughter near it your burnt-offerings and your peace-offerings, your flock and your herd; wherever I permit My Name to be mentioned I shall come to you and bless you. And when you make for Me an Altar of Stone, do not build them hewn, for you will have raised your sword over it and desecrated it" (Exodus 20:20–21). When God is reminded of swords, He regards this as a desecration and, one supposes, might withhold His blessing. For a family today that values the Bible and would consider bringing a gun into their home, this passage seems less than encouraging.

All which should leave us confused. The Bible's heroes were armed, but armament offends God. How can we make sense of these divergent themes in the Bible?

Sometimes an event brings questions like this into focus. As I was writing this book, I changed my mind about gun control. Tragedy is always the right time for introspection. It was the massacre of thirty-two students and teachers at Virginia Tech on April 16, 2007, that caused me to reverse a position I had taken in the past. That morning, a South Korean–born misfit, twenty-three-year-old English major Cho Seung-Hui, gave the most dramatic demonstration in American history of what guns in the wrong hands can do. The details of the event aren't the point, except insofar as they show how easily even a deranged person like Cho can buy weapons through licensed gun dealers. I admit I was wrong about gun control. On this, the liberals may be right.

I once held the view that the problem with gun control is it seems to assume that people lack the moral power to make free choices, so they can't be given the responsibility of owning a weapon. Whereas the properly biblical worldview emphasizes our freedom to act morally if we choose to do so, gun control advocates often seem to think it's a material object, a gun, that causes the shooter to commit his crime. A *New York Times* headline in the wake of the horrific morning in Blacksburg, Virginia, seemed to say it all: "Gun Rampage Is Nation's Worst," as if it were the Glock 9mm handgun that rampaged through an engineering building, while dragging the helpless suspect, Cho Seung-Hui, along behind it. A *Times* editorial put this even more clearly in its conclusion: "What is needed, urgently, is stronger controls over the lethal weapons that cause such wasteful carnage and such unbearable loss." There you have it. Weapons, not people, cause carnage. Could there be a clearer statement of mindless materialism?

In general, conservatives feel more comfortable holding people responsible if they make the wrong choice, rather than, in the liberal manner, never giving them the choice at all. That is one of the themes of this book. But when it comes to weapon ownership, I have migrated to the opinion that our culture isn't fit to be granted that kind of responsibility.

For guidance on public policy, I look to the Bible. Scripture encapsulates wisdom that you can think of as being either divine in origin, or simply the product of millennia of human thinking and experience brought to bear on ultimate questions.

At the same time, simply quoting a verse doesn't tell you how the biblical worldview would come down on a given policy question. The text is too cryptic and allusive for that. Instead, you need to see what the classic codifiers of biblical tradition say. The challenge is always to extract the general principle from the scriptural text and then to translate it into practical terms, applicable to the government of our public and private lives. That's what the Talmud does, as further clarified by legal codifiers like Maimonides.

As for the merchandising of weaponry, the book of Leviticus makes the essential point when it says, "You shall not place a stumbling block before the blind" (19:14). Obviously the verse isn't meant literally. Do we really need to be warned against tormenting the handicapped? No, it's telling us to take into account the weaknesses of a person in our dealings with him. Don't pour liquor for someone with a propensity to drink and drive. The verse doesn't contradict my previously stated principle that the Bible gives us liberty to screw up. But that principle is very broad.

There are certain circumstances—metaphorically speaking, conditions of "blindness"—where a society should act to remove temptations and causes for stumbling from before people who are likely to stumble. In its tractate *Avodah Zarah* (15b), the Talmud indicates how this would apply in a Jew's relationship with idolaters: "We may not sell to them weapons or accessories of weapons. Nor may we sharpen weapons for them. We may not sell to them stocks [for securing feet] or [prisoners'] collars, nor shackles, nor chains of iron." Maimonides codifies this as practical law in his *Mishneh Torah* (Laws of Murder and the Guarding of Life 12:12–14), forbidding the sale of "all weapons of war" or any "object that poses a threat to the public," and citing Leviticus 19:14. He makes an exception for selling armaments to the nation's military (or presumably its local police units).

That would appear to seal the matter, all right. Certainly from the perspective of Jewish law, there seem to be very solid grounds for restricting weapon sales. The only point of ambiguity arises from the fact that, to be precise, the Talmud in *Avodah Zarah* (meaning literally, "Foreign Worship") is concerned with "idolaters," heathens of a particularly nasty kind.

A spokesman for the National Rifle Association, if he were also a Talmud enthusiast, could respond: That was then. This is now. We don't live in the grotesquely immoral idolatrous society that the rabbis of the Talmud were familiar with. There is no analogy between selling a sword to their heathen neighbors and selling a handgun to our generally much more civilized American fellow citizens. My reply would be that it depends on how you define "idolater."

Many of the laws in *Avodah Zarah* haven't been applied for centuries. Partly, this is owing to the definition of idolatry advanced by an important medieval Talmudist, Rabbi Menachem Ha-Meiri, who lived in southern France. Ha-Meiri defined the characteristics of idolatrous and nonidolatrous societies—or as he put it, "nations not restricted by the ways of religion" and "nations restricted by the ways of religion." Provocatively, his definition of idolatry was based not on applying standards of Jewish religious dogma but on a more general consideration of whether the culture in question is secular or religious. A secular nation would be considered barbarous, therefore "idolatrous."

To the members of such a society, it would simply be too dangerous to sell deadly weapons. Being "not restricted by the ways of religion," such individuals should not be trusted with weapons.

On the other hand, living in medieval Catholic France, Ha-Meiri considered his own Christian neighbors to be "religious" rather than "idolatrous." To sell them armaments, for private or other use, would not violate the Talmud's rule. Nor at a biblical level would it be the equivalent of "placing a stumbling block before the blind."

The issue of gun control comes down, then, to a question about the nature of our society. Is it "religious" enough to merit free access to fire arms? Can Americans be trusted?

Some can, of course. But the Bible also advises, in evaluating the spiritual health of a society, that we look to the majority of citizens. A law in Deuteronomy (13:13–19) has it that if more than half of a city's population has embraced idolatry, it is to be considered a "wayward city" and destroyed. Because someone is bound to misunderstand what I'm saying, let me repeat. I am not calling for America's increasingly secular society to be subjected to biblical-style destruction. In fact there's good evidence that no "wayward city" was ever, in practice, identified and laid waste in Israel. Instead, the Bible is simply offering us a useful yardstick for judging cultures. It is saying there is a tipping point, beyond which the character of a society changes so much that new rules have to be applied in dealing with its population. Has America reached that point?

Conservatives prefer to think of the United States as a Christian country, which historically it certainly is. And indeed, according to the Pew Research Council, in 2002, some 82 percent of Americans, when asked about religious affiliation, claimed to be Christian. But I wonder how much that actually means.

Liberals and secularists will not like the direction I'm heading. But I also take note of a much more worrisome statistic from the respected Glenmary Research Center in Nashville. Their data are based on polling that asked people not merely how they identify but how they practice religion. As of 2000, the percentage of American "church adherents" stood at only 47.4 percent. If you add Jews, you get another 2.2 percent, for a total of 49.6 percent.

So Bible-believing Americans who actually practice a religion appear to be less than half the country. We should take that into account when deciding if ours is a civilized and religious society or, instead, an increasingly secular and barbarous one.

The tragedy at Virginia Tech by itself raises the question to which polling data and the wisdom of the Bible offer a troubling if tentative answer. God would vote to review our nation's laws granting such freedom of gun ownership, granting Giuliani, among others, his insistence that gun ownership, like free speech, is not an unlimited right. It is not something I relish admitting, but liberals may indeed be right about this. Just not for the reasons they think.

14

Privacy: I Spy?

Now that we know gun control is another way our biblically correct politics would depart from the libertarian conservative model, we may ask if there is any justification for what some would call a much greater departure. How about the National Security Agency (or other government bodies) turning aside the concerns of civil libertarians and gathering data on our phone calls in search of warning signs of an impending terror attack? That question held the nation's attention during the 2006 confirmation hearings of General Michael Hayden to head the CIA. Hayden, previously the director of the hush-hush NSA, attracted criticism from the Left verging on hysteria for his role as architect of the phone-data-gathering project. Are civil liberties a biblical value?

"The walls have ears." Rabbi Levi, a rabbinic sage and biblical interpreter who lived eighteen centuries ago, coined that ominous

phrase to explain the meaning of a verse in the Bible's book of Ecclesiastes: "Even in your thoughts do not curse a king, and in your
bedchamber do not curse the rich, for a bird of the skies may carry
the sound, and some winged creature may betray the matter"
(10:20). The author of the scriptural verse, traditionally held to be
King Solomon, sought to remind us always to be alert to the possibility of our words being overheard, including by spies of the state.

Solomon, who ruled over Israel at the height of her power and
prosperity around 950 B.C.E., was a realist if nothing else. As "king
over Israel in Jerusalem," he writes in Ecclesiastes, "I applied my
mind to seek and probe by wisdom all that happens beneath the
sky—it is a sorry task that God has given to the sons of man with
which to be concerned. I have seen all the deeds done beneath the
sun, and behold all is futile and a vexation of the spirit. A twisted
thing cannot be made straight; and what is not there cannot be
numbered." What he learned troubled him greatly: "For with much
wisdom comes much grief, and he who increases knowledge increases pain" (1:12–15, 18). Was Solomon hinting that the spies of
his own government brought back rumors and intelligence to him
of "all the deeds done beneath the sun" by the subjects of his kingdom, but that the more he knew of what his fellow men did, the
more this increased his own pain at contemplating the twisted nature of man?

Had modern high-tech surveillance technology been available to
him, Solomon could have appreciated the benefits of monitoring
the subversive activities of his subjects—subjects, for instance, like
his older half brother Adonijah who conspired secretly with disloyal
officeholders in the military and the priesthood to overthrow
Solomon. Ultimately, Solomon felt he had no choice but to execute
Adonijah preemptively, before the rebellion could be launched.

It's not hard to construct a case that the Bible holds privacy to be
an ideal. The book of Numbers tells of how after the Jews fled
Egypt and were camping in the wilderness, they were threatened by

a malign sorcerer, Balaam, who sought to curse them. Instead, the Lord turned Balaam's curses into blessings. Every time the magician sought to open his mouth and utter an evil imprecation, he found that he could speak only in praise of the Israelites. One of the blessings he uttered spoke ecstatically of the Jews' virtuous living arrangements. "Balaam raised his eyes and saw Israel dwelling according to its tribes, and the spirit of God was upon him. He declaimed his parable and said: '. . . How goodly are your tents, O Jacob, your dwelling places, O Israel' " (24:2, 5). What was so "goodly" about the dwellings of the Israelites? Though you would think the information would be worth mentioning, since the people are praised so highly for it, the Bible itself doesn't specify. Luckily the Talmud records an orally transmitted teaching. The verse means that the Jews arranged their tents so that "the openings . . . were not aligned one opposite the other" (*Baba Batra* 60a). That way, no one could spy on his neighbor.

Would God have a problem with the Patriot Act, the controversial piece of immediately post-9/11 legislation that Richard C. Leone calls "arguably the most far-reaching and invasive legislation passed since the Espionage Act of 1917 and the Sedition Act of 1918." He summarized the details of the law in an essay in his book *The War on Our Freedoms: Civil Liberties in an Age of Terrorism* (2003): "It allows the government to look at individuals' retail purchases, Internet searches, e-mail, and borrowed library books. It permits the U.S. attorney general to detain immigrants based on 'suspicion,' requires businesses to report 'suspicious transactions,' allows the government to conduct secret searches without notification, grants the Federal Bureau of Investigation and other agencies greatly expanded access to all sorts of personal business data with little judicial oversight, and allows for surveillance of any number of domestic organizations and advocacy groups." What seemed to upset people most about the Patriot Act was its Section 215, allowing our library records to be scoped out by government spies.

Meanwhile, statements from Bush and others in the administration have sounded ominously like justifications for invading our privacy in ways we may not even be aware of. As attorney general, Alberto Gonzales said before Congress that he was "not going to rule . . . out" domestic wiretapping possibly even without judicial oversight. Is it possible the ACLU's executive director, Anthony D. Romero, is on to something when he warns, with a note of panic in the words, "We cannot sit by while the government and the phone companies collude in this massive, illegal, and fundamentally un-American invasion of our privacy"?

King Solomon in his wisdom also said, "Whatever has been is what will be, and whatever has been done is what will be done. There is nothing new beneath the sun" (Ecclesiastes 1:9). While surveillance technology may dazzle us with its seeming novelty, while new forms of terrorism may dismay and confuse us, none of the issues considered in this chapter are truly new. They have all been dealt with before, as the Bible makes clear. Answers are there, in Scripture, if we look carefully.

Spying forms a motif in the narrative of Moses and his successor, Joshua. Admittedly it is not domestic spying that is at issue there. Still, there is a crucial lesson to be learned about the need for secrecy in intelligence-gathering.

Such secrecy, we're told by many on the liberal side of the debate, is in itself worrisome. In his book *Perilous Times: Free Speech in Wartime, from the Sedition Act of 1798 to the War on Terrorism* (2004), University of Chicago professor Geoffrey R. Stone notes with unease "the Bush administration's obsession with secrecy. Overbroad assertions of secrecy cripple informed public discourse. It is impossible for citizens to engage in responsible political debate if they are denied access to critical information about the actions of elected officials."

Moses would tell you somewhat differently than Geoffrey R. Stone. The great Lawgiver learned his lesson the hard way.

It happened in the episode of the spies, told in Chapters 13 and 14 in the book of Numbers. Moses sent them to reconnoiter the land of Canaan prior to the Israelite invasion he was planning. The spies were twelve princes of the tribes of Israel, dispatched with the full knowledge of all the Israelites themselves. When the spies returned, they spoke of the amazing qualities of the land, but also of its formidable inhabitants: "We arrived at the Land to which you sent us, and indeed it flows with milk and honey, and this is its fruit. But— the people that dwells in the Land is powerful, the cities are very greatly fortified, and we also saw there the offspring of the giant." The spies argued, "We cannot ascend to that people for it is too strong for us!" Unfortunately the report was delivered in full hearing of the populace, the equivalent of a nationally televised press conference. The people trembled, terrified, and wept all night long. They wished they had never left Egypt. They called for a new leader and the impeachment of the Moses administration. They appeared to have lost faith in the Lord.

It was an unmitigated disaster, and God took note, first contemplating wiping the whole people out for its faithlessness and starting over again with Moses, but finally relenting and agreeing merely to keep the Jews wandering in the desert for forty years till their children, and not the parents, would enter the holy land under Joshua's leadership.

After Moses had died in the plains of Moab, just on the other side of the border, Joshua led the invasion. First, however, he sent a pair of spies to scout out the situation in Canaan. Joshua had taken note of Moses's mistake in sending the spies publicly. The key to doing it right this time, he realized, was secrecy. "Joshua son of Nun dispatched two men—spies—from Shittim, secretly, saying, 'Go, observe the land and Jericho' " (Joshua 2:1). When they got back, they reported to him exclusively: "The two men then returned and descended from the mountain; they crossed [the Jordan River] and came to Joshua son of Nun and told him all that had happened to them. They said to Joshua, 'The Lord has given the land into our hands; and all the inhabitants of the land have even melted because of us'" (2:24).

What, however, about secrecy and surveillance when the privacy of the citizens themselves is at stake? I can think of three reasons why, if the context were national security, the Bible would grant leniency to a government to protect its citizens.

First, like Solomon, biblical tradition is suffused with realism. Recall the Solomonic warning about how "a bird of the skies may carry the sound" of your secret, "and some winged creature may betray the matter." One of Solomon's gifts, if you read the biblical text according to one interesting tradition, appears to have been an ability to speak with winged and other creatures, and with other living things: "He spoke *to* the trees, from the cedar which is in Lebanon down to the hyssop which grows out of the wall; he spoke *to* the beasts, *to* the birds, *to* the crawling creatures, and *to* the fish" (1 Kings 5:13; the passage appears in other Bibles as 1 Kings 4:33). The preposition I've highlighted, "to" (Hebrew, *al*), can also mean "about."

Talking animals and King Solomon as Doctor Doolittle—that's realistic? Not if the verse is *understood* literally. It's possible that what the Bible means is that Solomon had an intelligence network, a human one, that acted for him as the "bird of the skies" and the "winged creature" he alludes to in Ecclesiastes that betray matters of importance for state security to the authority that needs to know them.

In the Mishnah, the great rabbinic interpreter and sage Hillel had Solomon's wisdom in mind when he warned, "Do not say of a matter that it is impossible it will be heard. For in the end, it will be heard" (*Pirke Avot* 2:5). Anyone who thinks that in the real world there can ever be a strictly guaranteed right of privacy isn't living in the real world.

Second, the Bible understands that some crimes by their nature are secretive and that law enforcement must respond accordingly. Thus, religious law as rendered by the Talmud permits covert surveillance against the ultimate subversive in society: he who secretly entices others to worship foreign deities. As the book of Deuteronomy points out, such a person routinely uses secrecy to commit his crime: "If [he] will entice you secretly, saying 'Let us go and worship the gods of others'—that you did not know, you or your forefathers, from the gods of the peoples that are all around you, those near to you or those far from you, from one end of the earth to the other end of the earth—you shall not accede to him and not hearken to him; your eye shall not take pity on him, you shall not be compassionate nor conceal him" (13:7–9).

Do not conceal *him* from punishment, but you may and indeed should conceal other people *from* him—spies—in order to catch him in the secret act. That is how biblical tradition understands the proper strategy for dealing with an idolatrous enticer, a strategy alluded to by the seemingly extra word "secretly": "If [he] will entice you *secretly*." The emphasis on surreptitiousness is meant as a hint, directing those entrusted with the law to deal surreptitiously with the wrongdoer, if need be.

The Talmud goes into detail about how this should be done, advising that the enticer be lured into a room where two hidden witnesses lie in wait. A person whom he has previously sought to entice then asks him to repeat his proposal. If the suspect agrees and makes a pitch for paganism, the witnesses jump out of hiding and bring him to court for punishment. The Talmud notes, "We do not arrange [witnesses] to lie in wait to [apprehend] anyone else . . . except for this one," namely the enticer (*Sanhedrin* 67a). Admittedly, this would seem to forbid eavesdropping on terror suspects or those who aid them. But wait.

The danger posed by the enticer is exactly the threat posed by the modern terrorist. So in Leviticus, God describes the calamity that awaits the society that condones worshipping other gods: "I will destroy your lofty buildings and decimate your sun-idols, I will cast your carcasses upon the carcasses of your idols, and My Spirit will reject you. I will lay your cities in ruin" (26:30–31). Idolatry is a catalyst of mass destruction. In the biblical way of seeing things, the danger of allowing a spiritual subversive the freedom to incite others to follow him in his crooked path is the very same danger America faces from her enemies: another 9/11.

Third, the Bible can be flexible. In his law code, the *Mishneh Torah,* Maimonides summarizes the regulations that in the biblically based legal model would ordinarily make it difficult for the king or the court to act against suspected lawbreakers. This is for the protection of the innocent. That is why ordinarily, when lesser crimes are at issue, it is forbidden for the government to engage spies to detect domestic criminal activity. On the contrary, possible lawbreakers cannot be prosecuted at all unless they are first warned that they are under suspicion, by two witness. How do we know? Because the Bible is intent on establishing whether someone who does something criminally wrong acted intentionally or unintentionally.

Thus biblical tradition provides that a wrongdoer be warned. As Maimonides summarizes the highly formalized procedure, the witness declares to the individual committing the act: " 'Stop!' or 'Do not do it! For that is a sin and [by doing it] you become subject to capital or other corporal punishment at the hands of the court.' If he stops what he was doing, he is exempt [from punishment]. So too, if he says nothing or nods his head [as if in agreement], he is exempt. Even if he says: 'I know,' he is exempt, unless he gives himself up [of his own volition] to death by saying: 'Nevertheless, I will do it.' In that case, he is executed" (*Mishneh Torah,* Laws of the Sanhedrin 12:2).

Obviously this would make a conviction based on secret observation impossible. The witnesses must not only make themselves known to the suspect but also have a conversation with him, in which case he must virtually condemn himself. However, these requirements are lifted and thrown out when the crime is enticement to idolatry. They may also be lifted in case of an emergency threatening civil society.

When circumstances are dire, the executive branch (the king) may take steps beyond those outlined in the Torah's laws (see *Mishneh Torah,* Laws of Kings 3:10). Implicit in the scriptural stories of the ancient Hebrew kings, Maimonides finds the principle that a king may do what is needed "to repair the world according to what the times dictate . . . to establish authority and break the power of the wicked." The power granted to the king is not unlike that given to the American federal government by the Constitution to suspend the "privilege of the writ of habeas corpus," allowing imprisonment without charge or trial, "when in cases of rebellion or invasion the public safety may require it." President Lincoln took advantage of this provision during the Civil War, as did his Confederate counterpart, Jefferson Davis.

Are today's circumstances dire? Arguably so. It was because of sensitivities about the civil rights of Zacarias Moussaoui, the "twentieth hijacker" who hoped to join the other nineteen suicide attackers of 9/11, that the FBI decided not to seek a warrant to search his laptop computer for clues about a possible looming suicide hijacking in the works. The bureau's National Security Law Unit ruled that there wasn't enough evidence linking Moussaoui with a "foreign power," which would have been required to secure a warrant under the Foreign Intelligence Surveillance Act. So his privacy was respected and the attacks went off without a hitch.

Canada, of all places, appears to have learned a valuable lesson from this. When that country foiled a terror attack in June 2006, by arresting seventeen resident Islamists, it was thanks to domestic spying. As *The New York Times* reported, "Before making the arrests, the authorities spent months, and perhaps more than a year, monitoring [Steven Vikash] Chand and others, tracking them through Internet chat rooms, e-mail messages and telephone communications, Canadian and U.S. law enforcement officials have said. Only after the group tried to buy ammonium nitrate—a fertilizer that can be used to build a bomb—did officials intervene." The plot was to involve hijacking Parliament and beheading Prime Minister Stephen Harper.

Times change, but as even Canada seems to grasp, certain timeless principles remain. The Bible understands secret instigators of idolatry as the ultimate threat. If one urgent threat America faces is from secret instigators of terror, then Scripture's realistic counsel would be, in short, to be realistic. God would vote for a presidential candidate who would feel comfortable keeping someone like General Hayden on duty at the Central Intelligence Agency.

15

Censorship:
What Phinehas Saw

After 9/11, many of the classic moral issues on which the Right and Left disagreed came to feel passé, tired, tedious. Among respectable conservatives, especially the neocon variety, the new focus was devoted to fighting international "Islamofascist" terror, the assumption being that this would be the crucial arena of struggle for our country for the decade, or probably a good while longer. The idea has been the whole basis of Rudy Giuliani's campaign for the Republican presidential nomination. But the Bible always urges us to worry *primarily* not about external threats to our national welfare but internal ones, moral threats. Nowhere in Scripture does the ancient kingdom of Israel suffer because it was insufficiently focused on maintaining the security of her borders, as a matter distinct from maintaining a correct relationship with God through right action. When the Jews committed evils (idolatry, adultery, theft, and so on), that had ramifications for their security from enemy attack. At such times, God withdrew his protection from the country. However the enemy was not an independent danger.

In his 1996 book, *Slouching Towards Gomorrah,* in a chapter called "The Case for Censorship," Judge Robert H. Bork notes the "sexual incitement" committed by the performer Madonna. To worry about Madonna today, only twelve years later, seems almost quaint. Bork asked a woman who counseled unwed teen mothers about what she, the counselor, would do to address the problem of illegitimacy. The woman replied, "Shoot Madonna." In post-9/11 America as we know it, a book like Bork's would never be published. In a biblical America, confronted with the challenge of omnipresent Internet and other pornography, Bork's message would be considered right on target.

The politics of free speech has become confused. It once would have been obvious to all that the political Right favored censoring offensive material. By the same token, when a "free speech" movement arose in the 1960s, it was naturally from the student community associated with the Left. Today, as conservatives often complain, it is campus liberals who thwart speech deemed politically incorrect, because it is too conservative or too religious, while the task of standing up for the First Amendment is left to conservatives.

A biblical-democratic politics would favor what we think of as the *old* conservative view that not all words and images deserve the government's protection. If we divide controversial discourse into two broad categories—political and entertainment—we'll see that the Bible has much more tolerance for extreme expressions in the first than the second.

Scripture's most detailed portrait of a political leader is that of Moses. He led a couple million escaped slaves in the desert for forty years. During that time, he endured tremendous and abusive criticism from the mob of his followers, but he never struck back at dissenters. He would more characteristically throw himself down on his face in supplication before God but also before his critics.

Moses set a standard of humble leadership, followed by Israel's most beloved king, David. How tolerant of political dissent David was may be judged from an exquisitely painful event in his reign, the rebellion of his son Absalom. When Absalom drove David out of Jerusalem along with the dethroned king's loyalists, David was accosted on the road by a disgruntled member of the royal family of his predecessor on the throne, King Saul. This was Shimei, the son of Gera. Seeing David in a moment of weakness, Shimei not only cursed him publicly but pelted the king with stones, saying, "Go out, go out, you man of bloodshed, you base man! The Lord is repaying you for all the blood of the House of Saul, in whose stead you have reigned, and has given over the kingdom into the hand of Absalom your son. Behold—you are now afflicted because you are a man of bloodshed!" (2 Samuel 16:8).

David still had soldiers at his command. One of them suggested that Shimei for his insolence be beheaded on the spot. But David would not permit it, replying, "Let him be; let him curse, for the Lord has told him to" (16:11). Even after David was restored to rule, and after he was again urged to revenge his honor, he let Shimei live.

In our own modern American context, imagine a political opponent throwing stones at the president's motorcade. He would certainly be arrested. We take the president's safety, and his honor, very seriously. David was willing to forgo such concerns. Admittedly, once David was dead, his son King Solomon put Shimei under a liberal form of house arrest where he was not permitted to leave Jerusalem. The penalty if he violated this rule was to be, as Solomon made clear, death. Shimei, however, defied the order and traveled to Gath, not far away, on personal business. For defying the king's command, but not for his outspoken political views, he was executed.

We can thus dispense with any worry that in a biblical society, political dissent would be suppressed. How Hollywood and the pornography industry would fare is a different matter.

There was no mass media, no Internet, in biblical times. Porn, however, is no recent invention. The word goes back to a book written in 1769 by the French moral reformer Restif de la Bretonne, *The Pornographer.* The stuff was abundantly available in the Victorian age, but no historical period has been glutted as our own is thanks to the Internet. American political conservatives until very recently fretted volubly about the malign influence of television and the movies, with their graphic portrayals of sex and violence. But Internet porn, infinitely more extreme in nature as well as being available on your desktop at a moment's whim, has swamped Hollywood as a source of worry.

You hear mainly about the Internet as it impacts children—kids exploited as child porn models, kids being solicited by online predators, kids "mistakenly" discovering porno Web sites while innocently doing their homework research. However there is no less to worry about, and maybe more, in the less talked about area of "pornified" adults, to borrow the title of Pamela Paul's 2005 book, *Pornified: How Pornography Is Transforming Our Lives, Our Relationships, and Our Families.* Paul delves into the $14-billion-a-year porn industry, which takes in more money than all the most popular pro sports combined.

Your average man is, in a sense, addicted to sexual thoughts, which he may control more or less well just as any alcoholic may control that craving more or less successfully. Putting him all day in front of a computer with Internet access is a bit like asking an alcoholic to work with a bottle of Scotch and a tumbler full of ice always at the ready on the desk in front of him.

Can we hope to find anything in the Bible to help understand what society's proper response should be? The answer is as extreme, in its way, as the problem in need of addressing.

The closest parallel is in Numbers, the Bible's fourth book and one of its less often cited, possibly because of the uninspiring title as rendered in English translations. It is called that because Numbers begins with a census taken of the Jewish people at God's command. The Hebrew name, *Bamidbar,* "In the Desert," is more informative. One of the most fascinating books in Scripture, *Bamidbar* recounts the experiences of the Jews after they received the Torah at Sinai but before they entered the land of Israel.

One hero who appears there is the zealously moral Phinehas, a grandson of Moses's brother Aaron. The context is an episode in which a wicked gentile prophet, Balaam, plots to harm the Jews encamped in the desert by sending women from the neighboring countries of Moab and Midian to seduce the men and lead them to worship a false god called Baal-peor. According to tradition (hinted by the etymology of the god's name), the idol of Baal-peor was served by defecating in front of it, an act of perversion that would probably appeal to some Internet fetishists.

Tens of thousands of males from the Israelite camp succumbed to Balaam's plot. In the midst of this shocking and tragic development, one Jew, a tribal leader called Zimri, took the degradation a step further. Other men were enjoying themselves in private, but Zimri decided to make his sin public. "In the sight of Moses and in the sight of the entire assembly of the Children of Israel," Zimri paraded a Midianite woman called Cozbi, with whom he proceeded to copulate. The leaders of the people were reduced to "weeping at the entrance of the Tent of Assembly" (Numbers 25:6).

Much of this should strike a familiar note with us—the titillating vision of Zimri and Cozbi in their act, the ready availability to the whole "Children of Israel" of this image, and the moral leaders of the generation, paralyzed by inaction, crying helplessly. Nor is it as if the Jews who gave in to the seduction of the Moabite women, or Zimri himself with his Midianite lover, were marginal people. They were a sincerely religious group, having stood at Mount Sinai, no less, who had heard God's own voice there!

Balaam's plot was brilliant. He understood, as Americans once did, that order and prosperity depend on a certain minimum standard of domestic morality. With this in mind, in *Democracy in America,* Alexis de Tocqueville observed of our own country as it was in 1831, "In America all those vices that tend to impair the purity of morals and to destroy the conjugal tie are treated with a degree of severity unknown in the rest of the world." A really insidious enemy of our nation would send us Moabite women.

Into this scene of chaos strides the figure of Phinehas—in Hebrew, *Pinchas* (the "ch" is pronounced as in the Scottish *loch*). He was a member of the assembly of sages and elders, from whom, however, he separated himself at that moment. Without asking advice or permission from them, he stood up to take action, a spear in his hand. "He followed the Israelite man into the tent and pierced them both, the Israelite man and the woman into her stomach" (25:8).

Here it sounds like Zimri and Cozbi had actually gone into private to commit their sin. Whether the intercourse or just the foreplay was witnessed by all doesn't really matter. Phinehas acted because of the public nature of the crime, because of its demoralizing effect on the rest of the people. For this, God blessed Phinehas: "Behold! I give him My covenant of peace. And it shall be for him and his offspring after him a covenant of eternal priesthood, because he took vengeance for his God, and he atoned for the Children of Israel" (25:13).

Can such violence and zealotry be translated into acceptable modern terms? The advice to "Shoot Madonna" would be a rather literal translation of the Phinehas strategy, more so than most of us would be prepared to consider.

Luckily, arresting and executing entertainers and their distributors are not what the Bible advises us to do. One notable feature of Phinehas's zealotry is that he acts without Moses's consent. The Five Books of Moses are a work firstly of law, full of legislation appropriate for enactment by a government. No legal apparatus is being advocated in the Phinehas narrative. Indeed as biblical tradition has set down the practical implications of the story, in a discussion in the Talmud's tractate *Sanhedrin,* if a latter-day Phinehas were to approach a court to ask for their stamp of approval for some act of similar zealotry he was plotting, the court should not give him their approval.

Instead, we are being offered a strategy for overcoming moral paralysis. It amounts to the advice that we stand up as Phinehas did, never mind the weeping, helpless elders, and act. Let's start with the Net.

The Bible doesn't indicate what styles of porn should or (technically) could be filtered by the major ISPs under legislative order. In fact, any regulation could likely be evaded by Internet-savvy users. But recall the image of the alcoholic working with a bottle of whiskey before him. Let's at least remove the liquor from his view, though he may hypothetically retrieve it on his own by breaking open the locked liquor closet. Life has plenty of other temptations. Some porn users might even be grateful.

To this truly modest proposal, I foresee three objections.

First, isn't this the bad old way religion was in the Middle Ages, and still is in some parts of the world? The Catholic Church had its *Index Librorum Prohibitorum* ("Index of Prohibited Books"), from 1557 to 1966, banning morally, theologically, politically offensive works. Or should we go down the path of the Iranian ayatollah's 1989 *fatwa,* a condemnation to death, against Salman Rushdie and his publishers and translators for bringing out his "heretical" novel *The Satanic Verses?*

Some religions are to this day nervous at talk of censorship because of this history. Christian sages including Augustine and Aquinas favored compelling heretics to part with their heretical views, on pain of death. A biblical proof text for this was Luke 14 and the parable of the great banquet, in which the master (representing God) says, "Go out to the highways and hedges, and compel people to come in, that my house may be filled" (14:23). From this, Augustine derived that people may be compelled to "do right."

The obvious reply to the objection is that filtering the Internet is nothing that civilized secular countries aren't already doing, and we could too without going Iranian.

Second, doesn't this proposal go against the American way? When Bork wrote his book, conservative activist David Horowitz fired back a rocket fueled by historical misinformation. "In a democracy, the people are sovereign," cried Horowitz in his online magazine, wishing to argue that censorship is un-American. "If enough people find cigarettes, guns, and bad Hollywood pictures morally repulsive, these products will cease to be produced. That's the remedy the old-fashioned way."

Old-fashioned? Hardly. It was very recently that the idea even entered anyone's mind to apply the First Amendment to pornography. A 1942 Supreme Court decision, *Chaplinsky v. New Hampshire,* affirmed that the amendment's protection extends to ideas with "social value," not to the "lewd and obscene," and that the "social interest in order and morality" trumps any claim to protection that lewd materials might claim. Social critic Michael Medved also counters the "If you don't like Internet porn, don't look at it" argument: "To say that if you don't like the popular culture, then turn it off, is like saying if you don't like the smog, stop breathing."

More seriously than such objections, in this book I advance the argument that one thing that binds many conservative political positions, and grounds them in the biblical worldview, is that they presuppose individual moral responsibility. The Bible gives us

where animal sacrifices would be brought. In a great tragedy at the height of the priestly inauguration, Aaron's sons Nadab and Abihu went astray. On their own authority, they creatively offered a "strange fire" to God, an alien incense rite (Leviticus 10:1). When they did this, a fire issuing from heaven punished them. According to tradition, the fire entered their nostrils, incinerating their bodies, while leaving their clothing intact.

In the Bible, the punishment always fits the crime; so the fact that the fire entered their noses to kill them would suggest that in their sin, they ingested something through the same organ. I'm not saying they snorted cocaine, but a certain echo is there.

Their intention, no doubt, was noble. They wanted to come close to God by offering Him an incense service of their own devising. They were "high" in a spiritual sort of way. They evidently had used some sort of consciousness-altering drug, if not the incense itself, then alcohol. For just seven verses later, clearly as a response to the tragedy of the death of Nadab and Abihu, God instructed Aaron that none of his priesthood should approach God's service while intoxicated: "Do not drink intoxicating wine, you and your sons with you, when you come to the Tent of Meeting, that you not die—this is an eternal decree for your generations" (10:9).

Immediately, the Bible explains why the intoxication should be avoided: "In order to distinguish between the sacred and the profane, and between the contaminated and the pure" (10:10). That is, drugs blur reality, discouraging the making of proper distinctions.

In the spirit of making correct distinctions, let's divide the subject of controlled substances in half. Some substances—namely tobacco—merely boost your mood, improving your concentration, calming you down a bit, or picking you up. No more than that. At a grave risk to your health in the long term, of course. But smoking tobacco cigarettes, like drinking coffee, while you are under their effect does not change the orientation of your soul.

The only legitimate argument against cigarettes is a public health argument. That makes smoking bans one of the clearest illustrations of an argument I make throughout this book. Something that binds many liberal political views is that they discount the ability of adults to make responsible choices. To smoke is to recklessly endanger your own health. To spend lots of time around heavy smokers is also unhealthy. However, as most people with common sense recognize, secondhand smoke is dangerous in proportion to how much smoke you are in contact with and for how much time over the course of years.

Tending to your health is a clear case of individual responsibility. The Bible assumes we can exercise personal responsibility. It is a book of commandments. If we weren't capable of such self-control, it would make no sense for God to command us.

One reason, therefore, that liberals favor smoking bans more than conservatives do is that liberals and secularists are less likely than conservatives and religious traditionalists to assume that people can control their appetites for gratification. A biblical democracy would be wary of banning tobacco cigarettes if only to make clear society's commitment to the idea of personal responsibility.

We might add here that secularists are driven not only by their tendency to discount the importance of such responsibility but also by an additional, unconscious drive that the Bible recognizes. Recall the context of Nadab and Abihu's sin. The Jewish priests were being inaugurated for their service of God in the Tent of Meeting. That service consisted predominantly of animal sacrifice.

Does that sound unbelievably arcane and primitive? As the classical medieval sage Maimonides pointed out in his philosophical work *Guide of the Perplexed* (3:32), God commanded sacrifices in part because He recognized that the Jews of that era had a need to engage in such rites. They had been raised in the ancient Near East, after all, where worship of that kind was the norm.

Sacrifice remains a human need. The sociologist Rodney Stark has shown in his research that in the context of America's religious culture, churches have prospered—winning converts and members—when they ask believers to sacrifice—whatever it might be: their time (for example, through long church services), certain pleasures (for instance, premarital sex), or money (through tithing, giving a tenth of one's income to your church or to charity). Denominations that ask little of members tend to dwindle in membership. In the drive to ban smoking, we see the secular liberal will to sacrifice pleasures—so long as those pleasures are not legislated against by the Bible. If they were scripturally prohibited, of course, secularists would find a way to protect them. Such is the perverse logic of secularism.

All this analysis, however, has to be turned on its head when we switch our focus from cigarettes to mind-altering drugs. In the latter category, the Bible discusses only alcohol explicitly.

Travel back in time with me to the beginning of Scripture's narrative of human history. The Bible's first story of human interaction with the Lord concerns, of course, the first man and woman. Adam and Eve were placed by God in the Garden of Eden. They had the run of the place, with only one limitation on their enjoyment. God commanded that they abstain from consuming the fruit of a certain plant, the Tree of the Knowledge of Good and Bad (Genesis 2:16–17).

There are many misconceptions about this vegetation. First, it wasn't necessarily a "tree." The Hebrew word, *etz*, is ambiguous enough that Rabbi Meir in the Talmud (*Sanhedrin* 70a) transmitted an ancient tradition that it was not a tree at all but a grapevine. What Adam and Eve "ate" was in fact a beverage, wine. What is more, its source wasn't a Tree of the Knowledge of Good and *Evil*, as the phrase is often mistranslated, but of Good and *Bad*. The word "evil" implies a moral judgment. "Bad" implies a discrimination of taste or personal preference. Another classical medieval commentator, Rabbi Obadiah Sforno, clarified that before Adam and Eve sinned in drinking from the "Tree," they were different from later humans in that they perceived sin and evil as not only morally reprehensible but also personally distasteful. They could enjoy only what was morally commendable.

What a different world that was from our own. In the biblical perspective, wine is the archetype of a substance that, to us, tastes delicious but can lead to evil, by lowering moral inhibitions. Such a substance, to Adam and Eve before their sin, would have been perceived as—what else can one say?—yucky. After their sin, they had a new kind of "knowledge." Besides the knowledge of good and evil (as moral categories), they now had good and bad (categories of taste, preference, or aesthetics, independent of morality). This was the birth of secular ways of thinking, modes of analysis that do not automatically violate morality but—much more dangerous—leave it entirely behind. It was the beginning of secularism.

If wine was distasteful to Adam and Eve, why did the first couple drink it? The ancient Midrash (rabbinic interpolation) on the text explains that, like Nadab and Abihu, they were simply trying to get closer to God. Their tempter, after all, the wily Serpent, had told them that by consuming the fruit, "your eyes will be opened and you will be like God, knowing good and bad" (Genesis 3:5).

The Bible thus indicates to us the main danger of consciousness-altering substances. They hold out the hope of forcing a unity between people and God. More generally, a point that comes out in a variety of later biblical teachings, they fill our minds with illusions and untruths.

King Solomon is traditionally credited as the author of the book of Proverbs, which speaks urgently against drunkenness. "Wine makes a scoffer" (20:1), that is, one who "scoffs" at truth. "Do not look at wine becoming red, for to one who fixes his eyes on the goblet, all paths are upright" (23:31), that is, to the intoxicated person all moral values seem equally valid. Proverbs instructs that while intoxication encourages us to see ourselves as wise, the only way to acquire truth is through hard intellectual work. It must be bought with the currency of one's own effort: "Purchase truth," Solomon says, and "do not sell it—wisdom, discipline, and understanding" (23:23).

After the death of King Solomon, who ruled over a united kingdom of Israel, the holy land was split in two by a rebellion. The rebellious northern kingdom was called Israel, the southern kingdom, Judah. Sometimes, this rump state of "Israel" was also referred to as Ephraim.

In his prophecy, Isaiah decried the people of Ephraim. Ephraim's sins were highlighted by an overindulgence in alcohol. "Woe to the crown of pride of Ephraim's drunkards," moaned Isaiah (Isaiah 28:1). "Trodden underfoot will be the crown of pride of Ephraim's drunkards" (28:3). What was so damaging about Ephraim's indulgence? It produced errors of moral judgment: "For they, too, have erred because of wine and strayed because of liquor; the priest and the [false] prophet have erred because of liquor and were corrupted by wine; they have strayed because of liquor, erred in vision, perverted justice" (28:7).

Scripture was simply laying down a principle that would later be recognized empirically. William James, in his *Varieties of Religious Experience* (1902), makes the same point the Bible does. In the nineteenth century when, in Europe and America, self-medication was viewed as normal and healthful, he personally experimented with nitrous oxide and ether. In a neutral sort of way, he reported on the perceptions given when under their influence, especially their "power to stimulate the mystical faculties of human nature." He wrote that "drunkenness expands, unites, and says yes. . . . It makes [the user] for the moment one with the truth." Or so the user thinks: "This truth fades out, however, or escapes, at the moment of coming to; and if any words remain over in which it seemed to clothe it-self, they prove to be the veriest nonsense." Still, the "keynote" of the experience "is invariably a reconciliation. It is as if the opposites of the world, whose contradictoriness and conflict make all our dif-ficulties and troubles, were melted into unity." This results in "a monistic insight, in which the *other* in its various forms appears ab-sorbed into the One."

Adam and Eve were only the first to fantasize that they could be one with the ultimate *other*, the ultimate One, God. Most drug users and drunks just want a quick way to relax social inhibitions. But the really perilous promise held out by these substances is a blasphemy, the identification of the self with God.

Other abusers and addicts have contributed further confirma-tions, if unwitting, of the biblical insight. The occultist Aleister Crowley (aka "The Beast"), who died in 1947 and helped inspire the New Age movement, made a career of getting high. His biographer, Lawrence Sutin, mentions opium, ether, cocaine, heroin, laudanum, hashish, and anhalonium as the Beast's drugs of choice. It was all in pursuit of precisely the illusions that Scripture warns against. Crow-ley called them his "revelation," modeling himself on the New Tes-tament magical figure of Simon Magus. Sutin explains that in Crowley's twisted theology, "the magus dares to reach out toward the god by way of theurgy—high magic capable of influencing, and even merging with, Godhead itself."

In becoming like God, to quote the Serpent, one of the interest-ing by-products is that, conveniently, all the sins you wanted to com-mit become permitted. In the context of God, can one speak of prohibitions or sins? In Crowley's *Book of the Law*, which he claimed was dictated to him by an Egyptian deity, he "revealed" his great Code of Conduct: "Do what thou wilt shall be the whole of the Law."

So it goes. A depressing, disturbing continuum links alcohol, at the mild end, with still more dangerous ingestibles. The further up that continuum one travels, the more likely you are to fall into the il-lusion that Crowley did: that "truth" doesn't have to be "purchased" or worked for at all but can be smoked or injected. It's funny how regularly, with people who fall into this illusion, the anticipated "revelation" turns out to be an identity of the user with God and a Code of Conduct reducible to "Do what thou wilt." That is, do whatever feels "good." Obviously, if accepted widely in a culture, such a code would precipitate a descent to barbarism.

Anti-prohibitionists would overturn what God, apparently, in-tended. Believing in personal responsibility doesn't make you a lib-ertarian. Clearly there are some temptations that are too much to ask many people to withstand. God intended His world to be free of this particular temptation. When it comes to drugs, as a matter of public policy, America can't afford the libertarian approach.

But wait, what about alcohol? Doesn't what I have said so far lead to the inevitable conclusion that it too should be prohibited?

No—and I say this with relief and gratitude—it does not. Adam and Eve drank from the forbidden vine. There is no going back. Once the first man and woman were expelled from paradise for their sin, the way back into the Garden of Eden was forever afterward cut off and defended by fiery angels, *cherubim,* "and the flame of the ever-turning sword, to guard the way to the Tree of Life" (Genesis 3:24).

Simply, alcohol is the exception that proves the rule. Nor is its use in religious ritual, by Judaism and Christianity, an accident. When Jews employ wine, for example, in the opening rite of the Jewish Sabbath, the blessing over wine in the Kiddush, it is partly to remind ourselves of all the things that go with the introduction of wine into human culture. Wine, a vital culture symbol, is a moral warning. It reminds us that not all that is sweet is always good.

But its importance is not only negative. King David, in the book of Psalms, exquisitely details the splendors and consolations of earthly life, including "wine that rejoices man's heart, to make the face glow from oil, and bread that sustains the heart of man" (104:15).

It would be impossible to fully observe the Bible's commandments if you never drank wine. In the Pentateuch, God commanded the Jewish people to celebrate three yearly pilgrimage festivals to Jerusalem. They would literally celebrate. "You shall rejoice on your festival—you, your son, your daughter, your servant, your maidservant, the priest, the convert, the orphan, and the widow who are in your cities" (Deuteronomy 16:14).

Biblical tradition points out the seemingly superfluous listing of individuals being commanded here to "rejoice," namely "you, your son, your daughter," and so on. Scripture doesn't waste words. With this is mind, the Talmud *(Pesachim* 109a) transmits the tradition that we are meant to understand that each kind of person in the list has his or her own way of celebrating. For adult males, anyway, the "rejoicing" being commanded for the festival day can refer only to drinking wine.

A biblical America needs wine, and, it would seem, plenty of it. Be careful of excess, but otherwise enjoy. The same cannot be said of other substances of a similar consciousness-altering quality. A contradiction? Maybe. But God as a voter would feel at ease allowing that paradox to be expressed in laws that, following common sense, allow liberty to alcohol drinkers and tobacco smokers while directing the government's wrath against vendors of other drugs that more radically alter the orientation of the soul.

III

WORLD

17

Immigration:
Strangers Among Us

Forming a bridge between the national and the international, the permeability of our country's borders and the exclusiveness of citizenship have distinct religious resonances, as Democratic politicians have not been shy to point out. Hillary Clinton invoked the authority of Jesus himself to oppose cracking down on those who aid and abet the smuggling of aliens across the Mexican border. "It is certainly not in keeping with my understanding of the Scripture because this bill would literally criminalize the Good Samaritan and probably Jesus himself," Mrs. Clinton claimed.

Scripture speaks repeatedly of the kindness due to a "stranger" and reminds us often that the people of the Bible, the Jews, were once despised foreigners in an alien land, Egypt. So too were their forefathers, Abraham, Jacob, and Joseph, who were similarly compelled to live as immigrants in Pharaoh's land. Therefore to ask what immigration policies would be favored in our biblical democracy would seem entirely appropriate.

President Bush has advocated reforms that stake out a middle ground between the extreme positions of sealing the border with Mexico and expelling the 12 million or so illegals (if that were even possible, which of course it's not), on one hand, and opening the border without restriction, on the other. This middle position favors increasing border security, deploying the National Guard, while offering some immigrants "guest worker" status that could provide a transition to full citizenship. Such a position has offended some on both the Right and the Left.

While the political Left typically resists applying biblical insights to modern political problems, fearing the encroachment of the church on state matters, liberals have seemed to make an exception for this issue. Among notable clergy, the archbishop of Los Angeles, Roger Cardinal Mahony, has made this issue his own, citing the New Testament in support of granting legal status to currently illegal immigrants: "It is our Gospel mandate, in which Christ instructs us to clothe the naked, feed the poor and welcome the stranger."

He had in mind a passage in Matthew 25 describing the Great Judgment when the "Son of man" will blast wrongdoers with the charge that they failed to attend to the needs of society's most vulnerable: "Depart from me, you cursed, into the eternal fire prepared for the devil and his angels; for I was hungry and you gave me no food, I was thirsty and you gave me no drink, I was a stranger and you did not welcome me, naked and you did not clothe me, sick and in prison and you did not visit me" (25:41–43).

A Christian might also bring forward the teaching of Paul that after the advent of Jesus Christ the distinction between native and foreigner, Jew and gentile, has been transcended: "So then you are no longer strangers and sojourners but you are fellow citizens with the saints and members of the household of God" (Ephesians 2:19).

From the perspective of the Hebrew Bible, there are many verses one could quote that seem to advocate a wide-armed welcome for immigrants and foreigners. Here are a couple from Leviticus: "When a stranger dwells among you in your land, do not taunt him. The stranger who dwells with you shall be like a native among you, and you shall love him like yourself, for you were aliens in the land of Egypt—I am the Lord, your God" (19:33–34). "If your brother becomes impoverished and his means falter in your proximity, you shall strengthen him—stranger or resident—so that he can live with you" (25:35).

That last verse appears to teach that a "stranger" (in Hebrew, a *ger,* a word whose meaning we'll consider momentarily) not only should be welcomed and accepted but also supported and uplifted from poverty. So much, it would seem, for objections that illegal immigrants come to our country to enjoy the generous social welfare programs. Whether they really do that or not, doesn't it look as if the Hebrew Bible is telling us they deserve to take advantage of all the government benefits to which a "resident" or citizen is entitled?

Not so fast, actually. There is a problem with artificial cherry-picking of biblical verses to support the political cause of your choice. As indeed it is possible to do. This, in fact, has become a favored tactic among advocates of "spiritual activism" (as they are called on the Left) or "faith-based activism" (as they are called on the Right).

If we want to take the Bible seriously as a guide to crafting wise policies, that means taking the whole Bible seriously, rather than picking out only the bits we personally find congenial. It means trying our best to see Scripture as an organic whole with a unitary message. After all, if the Bible is only a treasure trove of beautiful and serious-sounding quotations from which we are free to choose according to our predilections—much as a writer of articles or speeches might make use of pungent quotations from Shakespeare's plays, while never bothering to wonder what Shakespeare personally would think of the issue at hand—then on what grounds do we regard Scripture as an ultimate authority, stamped with God's own wisdom? We don't view Shakespeare that way.

So let's try to take the Bible, the whole Bible, seriously while applying its wisdom to the immigration question. True, the Holy Bible on your bookshelf may speak in different voices. We could, for example, make a distinction between the Old and the New Testaments. But we are talking here, regarding immigration, about a classically political issue, and the Gospels and Paul's letters are remarkably nonpolitical. Not so the writers of the Hebrew Bible, a document that is very much concerned with the design of a just and merciful commonwealth.

So when considering an issue like immigration, even Christians are entitled to put the New Testament to one side for a moment and cast their eyes more to the Old. This is not artificial cherry-picking of Bible verses but rather the recognition of a dichotomy of perspectives inherent in the Christian Bible itself.

As for how the Hebrew Bible sees the immigration question, there are three major and pertinent observations to make.

First, unlike Paul, the Hebrew Bible insists on the continuing, eternal relevance of national identity. Even in the times of the Messiah, according to Isaiah's prophecy, the nations will not cease to exist. In that future epoch, when God's Name is recognized as One throughout the world, "the Lord will become known to Egypt, for the Egyptians will know the Lord on that day; and they will worship with sacrifice and meal-offering, and they will make a vow to the Lord and fulfill it." Will Egypt then merge into some generic, undifferentiated, European Union–style "humanity"? Not at all: "On that day there will be a road from Egypt to Assyria; Assyrian will come into Egypt and Egyptian into Assyria, and Egypt will serve [the Lord] with Assyria."

But as distinct peoples, even then. "On that day Israel will be the third party with Egypt and with Assyria, a blessing in the midst of the land, for the Lord, Master of Legions, will bless them, saying, 'Blessed is My people, Egypt; and the work of my hands, Assyria; and My heritage, Israel' " (see Isaiah 19:19–25).

In an illuminating essay in the journal *Azure*, "Locusts, Giraffes, and the Meaning of Kashrut," Rabbi Meir Soloveichik reflected on the relationship between the Torah's dietary code (*kashrut*) and nationalism. While scholars have debated the reasons for this institution, restricting Jewish diners from enjoying certain classes of tasty animals, Soloveichik points out that what seems to be God's own rationale for kosher food is given plainly in the Torah's text itself. Immediately after summarizing the command to distinguish between animals that may be eaten and those that may not, God says: "You shall be holy for Me, for I the Lord am holy; and I have separated you from the people to be Mine" (Leviticus 20:26).

The main purpose of the kosher laws is to remind us to make distinctions between classes—of animals and of nations. This doesn't mean there is anything unwholesome about a horse (nonkosher) as compared with a cow (kosher), but rather that we must always bear in mind that God created peoples and animals separate, with their differences, for reasons of His own. We noted this in an earlier chapter on affirmative action.

That there is such a thing as national identity, and that it matters and should not be treated lightly, is point one. Point two, however, is that the Bible sets up a standard, a demanding one, by which if a person wishes, he may shed one national identity and embrace another.

The classic instance is Ruth, the Moabite. According to the Bible, her time was one of "famine" in the land of Israel, a time not only of hunger for food, but also of spiritual malnourishment—much like our own time. A wealthy Israelite, Elimelech, his wife, Naomi, and their two sons fled for nearby Moab, a country known for its stinginess. There Elimelech would not feel so obliged to support the poor, as he had in Israel.

Elimelech died soon after, and his sons decided to intermarry, wedding a pair of Moabite girls, Ruth and Orpah. When the sons also died, Ruth resolved to return to Israel with Naomi. While the mother-in-law protested that Ruth would be better off staying put, Ruth responded with the beautiful and timeless declaration that she no longer wished to be a Moabite at all: "For where you go, I will go; where you lodge, I will lodge; your people are my people, and your God is my God; where you die, I will die, and there I will be buried. Thus may the Lord do to me, and so may He do more, if anything but death separates me from you" (Ruth 1:16–17).

Having "converted" to Judaism with this passionate speech, Ruth then returned with Naomi to Israel. There she remarried and became a key ancestor in King David's lineage. Biblical tradition to this day derives the basic laws of conversion from Ruth's overwhelming devotion to the people of Israel.

Ruth's is a pro-immigrant story—but with a twist that may make those on the amnesty side of the immigration debate uncomfortable. Thoughtful advocates of amnesty recognize the need for some standards. To become a citizen, you should have to learn English. But that's not enough. Professors James Q. Wilson and Peter Skerry (respectively of Pepperdine University and Boston College) provocatively advocate that as a precondition immigrants be required to do community service. That's more like it. If we are to follow the spirit of the Bible, as amnesty advocates have been advocating, then every new American should, like Ruth, need to demonstrate a commitment to patriotism and civic spirit.

One thing that shocked and dismayed many Americans about the 2006 demonstrations by mostly Mexican immigrants—including many who entered the country illegally and now wish to gain legal status—was the numerous Mexican flags displayed by the marchers. Would Ruth have flown a Moabite banner? My goodness, no. An utter, all-transcending commitment to her new people was her standard.

With such a personal transformation accomplished, Ruth becomes in almost every practical respect like any other Israelite: "For the congregation—the same decree shall be for you and for the proselyte who sojourns, an eternal decree for your generation; like you like the proselyte shall it be before the Lord. One teaching and one judgment shall be for you and for the proselyte who sojourns among you" (Numbers 15:15–16).

The subject of conversion isn't quite so simple, however. For there are actually two subclasses grouped under the category of the *"ger."* There is the *ger,* the convert, like Ruth—a full member of Israel who loses all affiliation with her previous citizenship identity and merges entirely into her new identity as a Jew. But there is another, the *ger toshav,* or resident alien. The latter occupies a middle ground between Jew and foreigner. It is this individual whom Jews are, in the verse we saw earlier, commanded to support and provide for: "If your brother becomes impoverished and his means falter in your proximity, you shall strengthen him—stranger or resident [*ger v'toshav*]—so that he can live with you" (Leviticus 25:35).

This resident alien too must fulfill criteria to join his new society, though the criteria are different than for a regular convert. While the precise standards are debated in the Talmud, Maimonides ruled that the "resident alien" must agree to certain basic moral propositions, including forswearing idolatry, murder, and sexual immorality. He is called a "resident alien" because it is only having satisfied this condition that a non-Israelite who doesn't formally convert may live in the holy land.

In translating the biblical ethos into contemporary terms, here then is the second point we need to keep in mind. The Bible invites us to admire and love a person who would give up his citizenship in a foreign country to join a new nation, our own. It also commands us to give material aid, whatever is needed, to any immigrant who agrees to abide by the moral law of the land. You might compare him to the "guest worker" in President Bush's proposed reforms.

However, and here is where the Bible may be hard for a modern reader to accept, scriptural tradition expects that any immigrant, any *ger*, will meet demanding criteria—basically, moral criteria. The idea that a sojourner would be allowed to live in the land without having accepted one of the two sets of conditions is simply unthinkable: "They shall not dwell in your Land lest they cause you to sin against Me, that you will worship their gods, for it will be a trap for you" (Exodus 23:33).

The Bible knows nothing of immigrant quotas. Theoretically, the land could absorb no end of worthy immigrants. But they must be worthy. If they aren't, it is a "trap for you," a moral one.

In practice, if applied, this standard would make it challenging indeed to qualify as a potential new American. Yet there is, in this biblical approach to the issue, nothing of the ugly nativism or racism that has marred past and present debates about immigration. There is nothing here of the romanticization of the "Anglo-American" past that you find in books by anti-immigration writers like Samuel P. Huntington, whose book *Who Are We?* (2004) bemoaned the threat posed by immigrants to the once regnant WASP culture that dated back to the seventeenth and eighteenth centuries. That makes the biblical view attractive. So too does the observation that this is not an unknown perspective in the context of American history.

Americans, and friends of America, have been worrying not about the race or ethnicity but about the morals of new immigrants since there was an America. Benjamin Franklin assailed England in 1751 for sending over morally unworthy foreigners: "Thou art our MOTHER COUNTRY, but what good Mother ever sent Thieves and Villains to accompany her Children; to corrupt some with their infectious Vices, and murder the rest?"

After the Civil War, opponents of liberal immigration laws were the same reform-minded Protestants who made a crusade, a moral one, against liquor consumption. For them, opposition to foreigners and to drunkenness were two sides of the same coin.

It was a later generation—nativists like Henry Cabot Lodge—that changed the tone of anti-immigrant rhetoric to a racial and biological one, resulting in the passage of the 1924 Johnson-Reed Act, which limited immigration on the basis of America's national origin makeup as it had been in 1890. This ethnic-racial-national standard was confirmed by the 1952 McCarran-Walter Act, and overturned only in 1965.

To judge foreigners on the basis of their racial origin would be anathema in a biblical America. The Bible's emphasis on moral choices to be made, by immigrants and natives, brings us to the third and really key point about the Bible's perspective on the immigration issue. Arguably, the most important word in Scripture is *mitzvah*, commandment. A mitzvah is given primarily to an individual. It confronts him with a moral choice. He will either make the right one or the wrong one.

The Bible, as we have seen, is much less interested in the government's making choices than in individuals doing so. In this, Scripture issues a challenge to the dominant political viewpoint today, which places moral responsibilities (feed the poor, house the hungry, free the oppressed) much more in government hands than in private ones. The Bible makes the assumption, a controversial one today, that individuals can handle the chance to choose right over wrong. We are morally responsible. In line with this view, it asks would-be immigrants to make a choice: either to choose citizenship, and zealously, like Ruth; or to choose to embrace fully a streamlined moral system. Either way, Scripture has enough respect for human beings to expect that we can make such a choice. It accepts no excuses, no whining.

To seal borders, or to open them without discrimination, would in either case be to reject Scripture's assumption of moral responsibility. Border-sealing would be a statement that we cannot realistically ask foreign-born individuals to choose our way of life and then expect them to live up to that choice. Conversely, to convert all illegals into legals and fling wide open the doors of welcome to all would similarly be to reject the Bible's insistence that we can set high standards and stick to them.

When Senator Clinton and Cardinal Mahony thump their Bibles in the name of liberalizing immigration laws, I hear no mention of setting strict standards for the new Americans we would thereby create. "What the church supports," writes Mahony, "is an overhaul of the immigration system so that legal status and legal channels for migration replace illegal status and illegal immigration." That is not the Bible's way. God would vote for immigration reform not entirely dissimilar from President Bush's failed attempts of 2005 and 2007; that would be too demanding for most liberals to accept and at the same time too welcoming for many conservatives.

18

Global Warming and the Environment: In Heat

We pass now from the human environment to the natural one. The biblical and the left-wing "environmental" views are in sharp contrast. So it has been startling lately to observe the way, on the issue of global warming, a sizable group of politicized Evangelical Christians have let themselves be recruited as key allies of the environmental movement.

In early 2006, eighty-six prominent Evangelical theologians and pastors joined together under the banner of the Evangelical Climate Initiative (ECI) to warn the world that "human-induced climate change is real." The signers of the ECI statement included Pastor Rick Warren, mega-best-selling author of *The Purpose Driven Life*. Citing the Golden Rule, "So whatever you wish that men would do to you, do so to them" (Matthew 7:12), ECI urges, "The basic task for all of the world's inhabitants is to find ways now to begin to reduce the carbon dioxide emissions from the burning of fossil fuels that are the primary causes of human-induced climate change."

Richard Cizik, the Washington representative of the National Association of Evangelicals, is well known for helping push Evangelicals in a green direction. When *Vanity Fair* published its May 2006 environmental issue ("A Graver Threat Than Terrorism: Global Warming"), one of the magazine's featured green heroes was Cizik, who, in an interview opposite a full-page photo of him walking on water, quoted the book of Revelation to the effect that God will "destroy those who destroy the earth" (11:18).

What is driving the present cultural contention about so unsexy an issue as . . . the *weather*? If human activities are modifying the natural environment with dangerous if unintended results, surely this is a problem that can be adequately addressed by scientists and other nonideological experts. Isn't it bizarre that conservatives and liberals have made climate change, that most prominent of all environmental issues, into a quintessentially partisan one, right up there with abortion, flag-burning, and prayer in school?

The problem is heightened when you consider that most reasonable observers, whether Democratic or Republican, concede that environmental degradation is a legitimate source of concern. In the summer of 2006, even as Al Gore was raising alarms with his highly effective global warming scare film, *An Inconvenient Truth,* President Bush agreed that climate change needs to be addressed. For that matter, John McCain has emphasized the issue in his presidential campaign.

It sometimes seems that the main point of disagreement between the major political parties comes down merely to *how* worried we should be, with Republicans advocating cautious concern while Democrats plump for outright panic, or as *Time* magazine put in an April 3, 2006, cover story about climate change: "Be worried. Be *very* worried." I will now explain why a biblical politics would encourage sober concern, but not more than that.

The historian Arnold Toynbee, writing in *The New York Times* in 1973, a few years after environmental consciousness sprang upon the public mind, viciously condemned the Judeo-Christian religious heritage for its supposed responsibility in degrading and polluting the natural world: "Some of the major maladies of the present-day world—in particular the recklessly extravagant consumption of nature's irreplaceable treasures and the pollution of those of them that man has not already devoured—can be traced back to a religious cause, and this cause is the rise of monotheism."

He pointed to two verses in Genesis. In the first, God blesses Adam and Eve, the first humans, on the day He created them, granting the pair dominion over the earth: "God blessed them and God said to them, 'Be fruitful and multiply, fill the earth and subdue it; and rule over the fish of the sea, the birds of the sky, and every living thing that moves on the earth" (1:28). That very day, however, the human couple sinned by eating the forbidden fruit of the Tree of Knowledge. God therefore expelled them from their home in the Garden of Eden, but not before setting the harsh terms of their new life. Having been parted from Paradise, Adam was told: "By the sweat of your brow shall you eat bread until you return to the ground, from which you were taken" (3:19). The man's right to "subdue" nature was not revoked, but it was coupled with the imposition of a fearful challenge to wring his living from the earth. From then onward, but especially following the Industrial Revolution, biblical religion encouraged a rapacious attitude toward the natural world. Humanity responded by decimating earth and sea in a quest for wealth.

This, Toynbee and later thinkers have felt, is in contrast with the much gentler and more admirable attitude encouraged by prebiblical and non-Western forms of spirituality. Because pagans stood in awe of the environment, they automatically conducted themselves with an appropriate restraint.

This may be an exaggeration of the classical pagan's supposedly meek, worshipful orientation to his natural environment. Consider the witness provided by the Roman writer Pliny the Elder in his *Natural History*, an encyclopedic summation of what was known about the world in the first century C.E. Pliny castigated his fellow pagans for their lack of environmental sensitivity in much the same vitriolic tone employed by Toynbee nineteen hundred years later.

Notwithstanding Toynbee, the Bible presents something very far from an open-armed invitation to all believers to come despoil the environment. Christians often speak of man as the "steward" of nature. The Bible itself uses the language of guardianship. In Genesis we have God placing Adam in the Garden: "The Lord God took the man and placed him in the Garden of Eden, to work it and to guard it" (2:15). In Hebrew the word meaning "to guard it" (*l'shamrah*) is the same language used in the book of Exodus in detailing the laws of custodianship. When one person appoints another to "guard" (*lishmore*) his property, there are various rules governing what happens if the guardian or custodian allows his friend's property to be stolen or damaged (see 22:6–12).

It's the same way with man in his role as God's appointed guardian over nature. The book of Deuteronomy forbids the wanton destruction of trees. This appears in the context of certain laws of warfare, where it is stated that an army besieging a walled city is forbidden to cut down fruit trees to build a bulwark: "When you besiege a city for many days to wage war against it to seize it, do not destroy its trees by swinging an axe against them, for from it you will eat, and you shall not cut it down" (20:19). From this seemingly narrow rule, biblical and Talmudic law derived a sweeping commandment in favor of nature conservancy. To destroy natural resources without strong reasons for doing so is to flout God's own will.

The reason given for God's forbidding us to swing an axe against the trees appears to make nature a mere vehicle for the fulfillment of human needs: "do not destroy its trees by swinging an axe against them, *for from it you will eat.*" Does this mean that the natural environment has value only insofar as it serves to feed, shelter, or otherwise please people? If trees offered us nothing, we could then cut them all down for any reason or no reason? How arrogant it sounds! In fact precisely that criticism is leveled against the Bible by some environmentalists. The Norwegian philosopher Arne Naess invented the concept of "deep ecology," emphasizing that man is very much a part of nature, albeit a destructive part. "The arrogance of stewardship," he has commented, "consists in the idea of superiority which underlies the thought that we exist to watch over nature like a highly respected middleman between the Creator and Creation."

Yes, it's true that Scripture grants "dominion" to man over the natural world: "You have made him but slightly less than the angels, and crowned him with soul and splendor. You give him dominion over Your handiwork, You placed everything under his feet: sheep and cattle, all of them, even the beasts of the field; the birds of the sky and the fish of the sea" (Psalm 8:6–8). On the other hand it is not so simple to say that all this natural splendor was created *for us.*

The book of Proverbs puts it this way: "Everything the Lord made [He did so] for its own sake" (16:4). Another possible translation of the same verse would be: "Everything the Lord made [He did so] for His own sake." Either way, Scripture is *not* saying God made it all *for us.* The Christian Scriptures echo this idea when Paul says of Christ that "in him all things were created, in heaven and on earth, visible and invisible, whether thrones or dominions or principalities or authorities—all things were created through him and *for him*" (Colossians 1:16).

When the Bible recounts the steps God took in creating the world, the six stages (or "days") of work, successive stages are capped in Genesis 1 with the famous exclamation of joy and approval: "And God saw that it was good." The first life on earth, vegetation, was "good." So was the first animal life. These things were good, complete in themselves, before God breathed a soul into the first humans on the sixth day. They were not merely "good" insofar as they served man's purposes.

The medieval rabbinic sage and philosopher Maimonides drew this conclusion, basing himself on a commonsense question: Could God have created man without also creating the earth and the heavens? Certainly He could have done so! God was not constrained to create animals, air, and water to nourish people. He could have designed us differently, such that we would need none of those things. So His decision to create the natural world as we know it was for some other reason than to care for or feed us. Why did He create such a splendid and diverse environment? Because it pleased Him: "It should not be believed that all the beings exist for the sake of the existence of man. On the contrary, all the other beings too have been intended for their own sakes and not for the sake of something else" (*Guide of the Perplexed* III:13).

This undercuts the usual anti-environmentalist sentiment that justifies man's doing whatever we wish with the nature around us, pillaging and paving it if that tickles our fancy, on the grounds that it was all made for us anyway.

God made the earth for its own sake. At the same time, He didn't make it to remain forever pristine and untouched by human hands. Part of the purpose of nature is to be settled and inhabited by people. The prophet Isaiah affirms this: "For thus said the Lord, Creator of the heavens; He is the God, the One Who fashioned the earth and its Maker; He established it; He did not create it for emptiness; He fashioned it to be inhabited: I am the Lord and there is no other" (45:18). The obligation to settle the world, not to leave it an empty waste, is considered to be so obvious and well understood by all that in Talmudic law, someone who fails to contribute to this purpose of God's—for example, if he idles away his time gambling, doing nothing to advance the cause of human civilization—is excluded from fully participating in civil society (*Sanhedrin* 24b). He is, for instance, forbidden to serve as a witness in a court trial.

The Bible's perspective on man's place in nature is balanced, in other words, in a way that makes radical environmentalism seem grossly imbalanced. Nature has absolute value, independent of any use man may put it to. On the other hand, God wants us to put it to use. When man changes the face of nature, this is not degradation. It's a divine mission.

What a contrast this is with the perspective of some misanthropic environmental activists who look on man as invader of nature, a hostile and alien force. That's the view of University of Texas ecology professor Eric Pianka. In 2006, on the occasion of his being named "Distinguished Texas Scientist" of the year, Pianka created a stir by denouncing humanity as a whole for having "grown fat, apathetic, and miserable" in the course of junking nature. The only solution, he declared, is mass death by disease, visited upon the "fat, human biomass." He hoped the Ebola virus would perform this valuable service, or alternatively, bird flu.

Among environmental activists, the view of humans as kudzu vine, in need of trimming and thinning out, is widespread. As the Sierra Club frets on its Web site, accompanied by a photo depicting teeming Third World masses, "Our planet is now home to more than 6 billion people—with a projected 50 percent increase in the next fifty years. The rate at which we consume and degrade natural resources jeopardizes the health of the planet and threatens the availability of clean water for generations to come."

✧

What exactly are we fighting about when we fight about climate change? Consider the Bible's famous story of environmental catastrophe: that of the Flood and its sequel, the Tower of Babel. God sent the Deluge to erase life and get a fresh start with Noah and his family. Later, a group of the children of these Flood survivors settled in the land of Shinar, saying to one another, "Come, let us build for ourselves a city, and a tower with its top in the heavens, and let us make a name for ourselves, lest we be dispersed across the whole earth" (Genesis 11:4). This plan greatly displeased God. "And the Lord dispersed them from there over the face of the whole earth; and they stopped building the city" (11:8).

What was so wrong with constructing the ancient Near Eastern equivalent of a skyscraper? The Talmud, in its tractate *Sanhedrin*, has an illuminating answer. When the notion of building a tower was decided upon, it was thanks to the collaboration of three groups of citizens. The first group said, "Let us ascend [to the top of the tower] and live there." They thought they could "live," survive the next flood, by propping up the heavens to prevent them from spilling forth their contents to drown humanity once again. The second said, "Let us ascend and worship idols." The third said, "Let us ascend and wage war." On whom? Well, who else resides in the heavens? They wished to wage war on God Himself.

When the call went out to construct the tower, few citizens had an inkling of what the most subversive in the society had in mind, which was to free humanity of God's rule. The sincere environmentalists were fooled into panicking about a nonexistent threat. For everyone should have been aware of the promise God made to their ancestor Noah: "Never again shall all flesh be cut off by the waters of the flood, and never again shall there be a flood to destroy the earth" (9:11).

Perhaps there is an implicit recognition on the part of today's

ment. They understand these sayings to be true and valid at all times and under all circumstances. When Jesus was born, says Luke in his gospel, angels broke into praise: "On earth, peace among men!" (2:14). In the Sermon on the Mountain, Jesus said, "Blessed are the peacemakers, for they shall be called sons of God" (Matthew 5:9).

Jesus and Paul both spoke about not resisting enemies: "Do not resist one who is evil. But if any one strikes you on the right cheek, turn to him the other also" (Matthew 5:39). "Love your enemies, do good to those who hate you" (Luke 6:27). "Repay no one evil for evil, but take thought for what is noble in the sight of all. If possible, so far as it depends upon you, live peaceably with all" (Romans 12:17–18).

But if the matter were so clear as the American Friends Service Committee or the Mennonite Central Committee would have us think, then how are we to explain the long tradition of Christian militancy? True, in the early church, until the reign of the emperor Marcus Aurelius (160–180 C.E.), we find no record of Christians joining the Roman military. The theologian Origen argued that a Christian's best weapon was prayer.

With the conversion of the Emperor Constantine (324 C.E.), all that changed. Church thinkers wrote of the concept of *kerygma,* warfare justified on the grounds that it spread the gospel to unbelievers—we might call it "holy war," or perhaps *jihad.*

The Roman Empire in the west fell but was revived, in name, with the coronation of Charlemagne as Holy Roman Emperor in 800— symbolizing a most pointed insistence that the work of empire, which meant war-making, was naturally at one with the work of religion. A Christian *jihad* was formally declared two centuries later by Pope Urban II at the Council of Clermont on November 18, 1095. The First Crusade, as it is more familiarly called, was defensive in nature. Byzantine Christian control of the holy land had been wrested by the sudden onslaught of a new religion, the Arab empire of Islam, after which Seljuk Turks had seized Palestine from the Arabs, along with all of formerly Christian Asia Minor (now Turkey). From the seventh century to the tenth, Islam surged closer and closer to Europe itself. Christians were terrified of what future decades and centuries might hold. The farsighted Pope Urban tried to halt the Muslim tide, but this came at the expense of extraordinary carnage. On June 13, 1099, the Crusaders took Jerusalem, standing in "blood up to their knees and bridle reins" in the ruins of the Temple of Solomon, as a contemporary Christian account recalled.

So it has gone down through the centuries. After decapitating King Charles I, Oliver Cromwell, on January 30, 1649, the self-styled "Lord Protector" of the Commonwealth of England, notoriously led the slaughter of some three thousand men, women, and children at Drogheda. He assured Parliament that it was God's will.

Cromwell's Puritanism, which regarded itself as following in the footsteps of the Israelites of the Bible, those ancient warriors, was imported to the New World. Yet the Puritan founders of the Massachusetts colony were of two minds about warfare. In 1675, the Indian chief King Philip commenced a terror campaign against the settlers, leading to the bloodiest war—measured in terms of casualties per capita—in American history. Some Puritans, such as the Reverend Increase Mather, argued that the only appropriate defense was repentance, prayer, and fasting. Others, like Samuel Nowell in his 1678 sermon "Abraham in Arms," strongly disagreed. Nowell pointed to the example of the biblical Abraham. When invading armies kidnapped his nephew Lot, the patriarch gathered his own force and went to war (Genesis 14). This line of reasoning was taken up and embellished by American preachers before and during the Revolution. Scholars who have studied the sermons from that era know how passionately, and beautifully, the American clergy preached the Christian duty of warfare.

This robust tradition of faithful militancy found a deliciously pungent spokesman in General George S. Patton. In his memoir *War as I Knew It,* he recalls the Battle of the Bulge in 1944, when the

American assault on Germany was bogged down in mud, rain, and snow. Patton ordered the chaplain of the Third Army, Monsignor James O'Neill, to compose a war prayer. O'Neill balked—"May I say, General, that it usually isn't a customary thing among men of my profession to pray for clear weather to kill fellow men." But Patton rebuked him soundly: "Chaplain, are you teaching me theology?" The prayer was duly composed and handed out to the entire Third Army, beseeching the "Almighty and most merciful God" for victory, so as to "crush the oppression and wickedness of our enemies." A day later, the weather changed, remaining clear as a bell for the next six days.

But what about not resisting evil, and turning the other cheek? Much confusion has followed when Christians failed to understand the context of these sayings, both the ethical and the textual.

The ethical context has to do with whether you think Jesus and Paul were speaking to private persons in their daily lives or to government policy planners. If Jesus meant to advise governments not to resist evil, then we immediately run into the problem of Christian tradition. Augustine in his *City of God* soberly accepted war as a "stern necessity": "it is beneficial that the good should extend their dominion far and wide, and that their reign should endure. . . . This is for the benefit of all, of the subjects even more than the rulers."

He began writing his great work in 413, three years after barbarians sacked the city of Rome. The Roman Empire in the east still survived with its capital at Constantinople. Augustine's theorizing about Bible and empire would fundamentally influence Christian thinking for millennia. "Peace," he wrote, "is the end sought for by war. . . . It is therefore with the desire for peace that wars are waged." Building on Augustine, Thomas Aquinas in his *Summa Theologica* laid down three criteria for the "just war": (1) it must be fought by a legitimate government; (2) the enemy must "deserve it";

(3) the just warriors must "intend the advancement of good, or the avoidance of evil." These three requirements don't seem particularly hard to satisfy.

Actually, it's evident that the evil Jesus had in mind was not that of wicked regimes but the insults and injuries we suffer in our daily lives from thoughtless co-workers and employers, friends and strangers, husbands and wives. The key difference between resisting evil from states and resisting it from other individuals is that when you turn your cheek to another person who has insulted you, the honor or interest you are treating lightly is your own. When you ignore the pain suffered by other people subjected to an evil regime, calling for a "peace" that would allow their rulers to go on oppressing them, that's different. Ignoring other people's hurt is easy—temptingly, seductively so.

In one revolutionary-era sermon, in 1773, the Massachusetts preacher Simeon Howard made exactly this point: "When our Savior forbids us to resist evil, he seems to have had in view only small injuries, for such are those he mentions in the following words, an illustration of the precept; smiting on the cheek, taking away one's coat, or compelling him to go a mile. . . . But it does not follow, that because we are forbidden to resist such slight attacks, we may not defend ourselves when the assault is of a capital kind."

That's the ethical context of Jesus's sayings on peace. There is a textual one too, that of the Hebrew Bible. On the subject of war, Christian thinkers have often cited the sacred history of the ancient Jews.

When Pope Urban commissioned his crusaders, he also did so by offering to them the example of Moses. The Jewish lawgiver fought the supernaturally wicked tribe of the Amalekites, against whom God (in the book of Exodus) had vowed to "maintain war from generation to generation" (17:8–16). The Pope saw his own role as a spiritual one, which included giving marching orders like this: "It is our duty to pray, yours to fight against the Amalekites. With Moses, we shall extend un-wearied hands in prayer to Heaven, while you go forth and brandish the sword, like dauntless warriors against Amalek."

The Hebrew Bible indeed gives a strong impression of viewing war as normal statecraft. Never mind that *shalom,* "peace," is the only Hebrew word your typical American bar mitzvah boy or bat mitzvah girl can reliably recognize and translate. War is deeply Jewish.

Begin with the way Hebrew Scripture defines the role of government—basically, to make war and execute justice. As told in the books of 1 and 2 Samuel, after centuries of being governed by judges, the Jewish people demand a sovereign ruler. They cry, "Our king will judge us, and go forth before us, and fight our wars!" (1 Samuel 8:19). The nature of executive government, the centrality of war-making to it, is taken for granted.

Later Jewish law would make the role of government crystal-clear. Maimonides concludes his summation of Jewish teaching, the *Mishneh Torah,* with a section called "Laws of Kings and Their Wars." "The purpose of appointing a king," writes Maimonides, "is only to execute justice and wage wars." Some of the laws of war may alarm modern readers. In fighting a defensive war, the king is granted enormous leniency. He must first offer peace to the enemy, defined as total surrender. But once this has been rejected, the king needs nobody's permission, not even the United Nations', to enter into combat.

When the war is not, strictly speaking, defensive, he consults the ancient legislative branch of government (the Sanhedrin). With their agreement, he is again free to act with few restraints, provided that all his deeds are for the sake of Heaven. Basing himself on Deuteronomy (20:13), Maimonides dismisses any quibbles about the distinction between combatants and noncombatants. Enemy males may be in or out of uniform, a point that would resonate with soldiers who have fought terrorist-guerrillas dressed as civilians: "All males past the age of majority should be killed."

In Jewish biblical tradition, offense is understood as smart defense. Sometimes, a campaign to intimidate enemies may work by intimidating dangerous third parties whom you aren't even making war on. When, under the prophet Samuel's leadership, the Jews waged a successful campaign against the Philistines, the Bible immediately notes: "and there was peace between Israel and the Amorites" (1 Samuel 7:14)—a totally different foreign aggressor nation. The Amorites saw what Israel did to the Philistines, and decided to make themselves inconspicuous.

If the Jewish Bible is Pattonesque in its comfort with warmaking, what are we to make of Hebrew Scripture's emphasis on seeking peace: "Turn from evil and do good, seek peace and pursue it" (Psalms 34:15). What exactly does "peace" mean?

Not, it would seem, merely a willingness to put down your gun or sword. Etymologists link the Hebrew *shalom,* "peace," with the ancient Akkadian word *salamu,* which means "to be whole, complete." In modern Hebrew, the related noun *shalem,* built on the same root, SHLM, as *shalom,* also means "whole, complete." As a verb, in biblical Hebrew, the root SHLM means to pay someone his due, to render him "complete" in the sense of giving him his just payment (see, for example, 1 Samuel 24:20 *"y'shalmechah"*). "Peace" is thus tied up with "justice," as in the famous admonition, "Justice, justice you shall pursue" (Deuteronomy 16:20), which has to do with the appointment of law-abiding court officials and police officers.

Peace comes only when the demands of justice have been met. This helps us understand some of the most beloved sayings of the Hebrew prophets. Isaiah promised, "They shall beat their swords into plowshares and their spears into pruning hooks; nation will not lift sword against nation and they will no longer study warfare" (2:4). The verse appears on a bronze statue at the United Nations in New York, depicting a man beating a sword into a farming implement, a 1959 gift from the peace-loving Soviet Union. Isaiah's words are immediately preceded by the promise that a Messianic king "will judge among nations, and will settle the arguments of many people." Justice, and then peace.

This is why the prophets are full of stark depictions of the wars that will accompany the Messiah's coming. First that awesome king "will strike [the wicked of] the world with the rod of his mouth, and with the breath of his lips he will slay the wicked"—and *then,* two verses later, "The wolf will live with the sheep and the leopard will lie down with the kid" (11:6). A "peace" that does not satisfy God's will to see evil rooted out is not true peace.

The biblical position may be summarized in the words of an ancient Latin proverb, *"Si vis pacem, para bellum"*—"If you wish for peace, prepare for war." The resistance of pacifists to that view has a long lineage. Very recently, however, there has emerged a consensus among Americans and Europeans on the Left that plays a novel variation on the old-style pacifism. The default position of the new antiwar thinking holds the seemingly paradoxical view that while war never solved anything (as if Hitler had not been defeated in World War II), nevertheless nations may take up arms with the consent of international opinion. An "illegal" and immoral war, waged without United Nations approval, would have been rendered legal and thus, presumably, moral had only the representatives of Uganda and Syria, along with France and Germany, given their blessing.

Thus, even more than the war itself, what seemed to bother Christian critics of the Iraq conflict was that America had decided to go it alone, without unambiguous U.N. backing. As Methodist general secretary Winkler put it, "This matter can and should be dealt with by the United Nations. . . . No member nation has the right to take unilateral military action without the approval of the U.N. Security Council." Which was not far removed from the position of 2004 Democratic presidential contender John Kerry, a Catholic. Kerry stressed the need for international involvement:

"Moving forward, the administration must make the United Nations a full partner responsible for developing Iraq's transition to a new constitution and government." He complained of how, in Iraq, "we are going it almost alone."

Winkler and Kerry felt America should seek guidance from an international body—let them decide for us! Oh, the lure of this idea, the wish to abdicate responsibility to others.

But neither Judaism nor Christianity makes sense without the individual moral actor—a person or a country—taking responsibility for himself or itself. As I've noted repeatedly, the moral system of the Bible may be summed up by one Hebrew word—*mitzvah,* or "commandment"—in which the individual receives God's commands, through the medium of revelation and tradition, and decides whether or not he will comply. Christianity too is premised upon personal responsibility. One thing Jesus never did was shrink from the implications of the moral authority he assumed. Even to his death, he took responsibility for himself.

Perhaps a tremulous follower scolded him: "But you could be wrong! You could die! You could cause others to die! Are you up for hanging such a heavy weight around your neck?" A national leader who resolves to make war, whether or not that decision proves in the end to have been right, is up for it. In making such a decision he implicitly affirms a moral premise—the individual as moral actor—that is among the most fundamental in the Bible.

Does this mean America should be fighting in Iraq at this very moment? Of course it doesn't mean that. Only a fool would look for a precise timetable for withdrawal of U.S. forces from Mesopotamia somehow encoded in Scripture. Indeed, God might very conceivably altogether disapprove any particular war you'd care to name—that's the whole point of undertaking morally responsible acts. But war in general, as a concept, He decidedly approves. A would-be political leader who fails to understand that basic point shouldn't seek God's endorsement.

20

Islamic Terror: Call Them Ishmael

After 9/11, the subject of the last chapter, war, cannot be separated from the subject of terror. Yet before considering radical Islam and the danger it poses, we need to put the problem in perspective.

Early in the 2008 presidential campaign, Rudy Giuliani's candidacy polarized politically conservative Christians and Jews—less over his liberal position on abortion than, more subtly, over a question of emphasis. On one side of the dispute: Jewish neoconservatives, tough on Islam, making up more than half the star members of Giuliani's foreign-policy advisory team. They emphasized the importance of aggressively confronting the Iranian regime. On the other side: Christians who said they would not rule out supporting a third-party candidate if Giuliani got the nomination. The Christians wished to emphasize the suite of pre-9/11 culture war issues, abortion above all.

Whatever else there may be to say in favor of Giuliani, on biblical grounds the Christian conservatives were right, the neocons wrong.

Ironically, no one should know this better than neocon elder statesman Norman Podhoretz, an enthusiastic Giuliani backer and author of the influential 2007 book *World War IV: The Long Struggle Against Islamofascism.* To judge from his excellent 2002 book *The Prophets,* Podhoretz takes the Bible deeply to heart. A radio host who's also Jewish told me that after a warm and stimulating broadcast interview with Podhoretz, the older man spontaneously blessed him with the ancient Hebrew priestly blessing given by Jewish parents to their children on the Sabbath eve (Numbers 6:23–27). When I heard that story, I got choked up.

Would Isaiah, Jeremiah, and Ezekiel shelve moral questions such as abortion in order to pursue an aggressive defense against Islamic enemies? In *The Prophets,* Podhoretz hammers away at one great theme: the prophets and their struggle against idolatry. Isaiah, Ezekiel, and Jeremiah had, as their overriding goal, freeing the Jewish people from a tendency to revert to idolatry and paganism.

Idolatry manifests itself in every age. Its essence lies in setting up moral authorities in competition with, or to the negation of, God. Today, aggressive secularism possesses all of the classic pagan hallmarks: relativism, nature worship, sexual corruption, and a willingness to sacrifice children for the cause.

The key point in Podhoretz's inspired treatment of the prophets is the way they invariably prioritized the struggle against idolatry over every other struggle. Keep in mind that they lived in a time of horrible danger from foreign enemies, much more so than we do. Today, Muslim political potency has been fading for centuries, notwithstanding obviously delusional dreams of establishing a global Caliphate. By contrast, ancient Israel, over several centuries, faced foreign empires (Assyria, Babylon) at the height of their power. Those two nations wiped the Jewish commonwealth out of existence. Yet the prophets had little to say against Assyrofascism or Babylofascism. They focused squarely on admonishing their own people to correct moral and spiritual failings. Theirs was a war primarily against internal corruption. They knew that if the Jews were right with God, He would protect them from external enemies.

Podhoretz, in *The Prophets,* expresses the point as well as anyone could. Consider Jeremiah, who lived through the sacking of Jerusalem and the leading away of her people to captivity by the empire of Babylon. He warned that, in the context of Israel's corrupt moral culture, it was useless to resist Babylon. For this, he was accused of treason by the war party among his fellow Jews.

He taught that purifying the culture was the real priority, of which the defense against Babylon was merely a secondary expression. Writes Podhoretz: "It is idolatry, and nothing else, that to [Jeremiah] is the cause of the catastrophe looming ahead." The prophet admonished in God's name: "And I will make Jerusalem heaps, and a den of dragons; and I will make the cities of Judah desolate, without an inhabitant." Why did the Lord propose to do this? "Because they have forsaken my law which I set before them, and have not obeyed my voice, neither walked therein; but have walked after their imagination of their own heart, and after Baalim, which their fathers taught them" (9:11–14).

Responding preemptively to Islamic terror—from al Qaeda or Iran—remains a necessary and prudent objective. A serious presidential contender must have a plan for it. But neglecting the country's internal moral landscape to fight "World War IV" is neither responsible nor wise.

None of what I have just said, of course, should be taken to mean that confronting radical Islam violates biblical principles. How, from a scriptural perspective, should we think about Muslims? That is the larger question to which I address this chapter.

The Iraq War was premised upon the idea that Muslim culture can be redeemed, freed from the obsessions many of its believers have with death and destruction. President Bush has sustained many fierce verbal blows from critics of his stance toward Islam, including from both liberals and conservatives who feel that the Muslim faith is hopeless—or "borderline Satanic," in the phrase of right-wing firebrand Ann Coulter. Many conservatives delight in mocking the president's designation of Islam as a "religion of peace." Can, in fact, any faith associated with the Arab peoples ever be anything other than a faith in gruesome violence?

The Bible turns out to have covered this ground, hinting at the future of Western-Islamic relations centuries long before Muhammad was born or the Koran was written, and providing a still relevant model of how to think about the Arabian-born religion and its many seemingly dysfunctional features. A biblical politics would not despair for the culture of Islam, nor would it rule out using war as a tool in speeding the religion's reform.

The hope that the Muslim world can be liberalized goes back more than two hundred years, to Napoleon's invasion of Egypt in 1798. Like George Bush, Napoleon made every effort to be culturally sensitive. He didn't want to establish a French dictatorship but rather to turn over government powers to the Egyptians themselves. He fully expected that, once exposed to superior European political institutions, the Egyptians would have little trouble melding Islam with liberal enlightenment. The historian Alan Moorehead recounts in his book *The Blue Nile*: "At banquets he sat cross-legged among the sheikhs and ate with his fingers. Each guest on one occasion found a copy of the Koran and of [Tom Paine's] *The Rights of Man* beside his place."

Bonaparte's adventure disintegrated as the French occupation was met with guerrilla warfare, under cries of *jihad* against the

Christian invaders. It took a push from England to get Napoleon's army out of the country, in 1801, with nothing positive having been accomplished by the invasion.

America too has taken the chance that Islam can be redeemed. We conquered Iraq with the stated purpose of seeking weapons of mass destruction in Saddam's hands. But the broader justification for the war was based on the argument that America would be safer from attack if we could democratize the Middle East. This is what we may call the optimistic way of thinking about Islam. If the optimists are right, then the way to fight terror may well be to declare war on Muslim despots as we did the despots of Germany, Italy, and Japan in World War II. This could ultimately allow, years down the road, a renaissance of the Islamic world as World War II allowed such a rebirth of Germany, Italy, and Japan.

If the pessimists are right, America can only hope to wall herself off from the terrorists. Alternatively, we can view the struggle as basically a police matter, to be tackled not by the U.S. military but by intelligence branches led by the FBI and CIA. But we can no more "win" a war against radical Islam than domestic society can ever hope to "win" a "war" on crime in general.

The Bible helps address this fundamental disagreement.

To begin with, Scripture encourages us to think civilizationally, somewhat in the manner of Samuel Huntington's 1996 book, *The Clash of Civilizations and the Remaking of World Order.* That is, to conceive of the world not as a collection of individual countries but as a mosaic of a much smaller number of civilizations, each of which includes many countries. While these countries may come and go, rise and fall, changing names and forms of government, the civilization that they together comprise remains—a far longer lived entity.

The Bible teaches us to think this way in a series of passages, mostly in Genesis, that many readers skip over as if they were of no importance. I refer to those extended genealogies of names, with one generation "begetting" the next, as in, "And Mizraim begot Ludim, Anamim, Lehabim, Naphtuhim, Pathrusim, and Casluhim, whence the Philistines came forth, and Caphtorim" (Genesis 10:13–14). These genealogical tables explain the interrelationship of world civilizations. Each obscure name represents a shared culture or peoplehood.

A critically important example comes in Genesis 10, which lists a total of seventy primordial nations. These are the building blocks of civilizations, of which, in the biblical perspective, there are basically three major ones: Shem, Ham, Japheth. We met them in an earlier chapter about race and affirmative action.

Those three names designate the three sons of Noah, who survived the great Flood that wiped out humanity ten generations after Adam and Eve. Genesis lists seventy of their descendants, noting: "These are the families of Noah's descendants, according to their generations, by their nations; and from these the nations were separated on the earth after the Flood" (10:32).

Few if any of these "nations" are recognizable today. Rather, they represent something like cultural genes, persistent tendencies that comprise the larger civilizations that indeed survive. The civilization of the Arabs gave the world Islam. In modern cultural studies, the Arabs are included under the linguistic and ethnological heading of "Semites." The term "Semite" means literally "a descendant of Shem." Arabs, as well as Jews, are equally considered Semites. That is because Shem had a descendant, Abraham, the biblical patriarch. Abraham's firstborn son was Ishmael.

In the Bible, his story goes like this: Abraham and his wife, Sarah, were very old and Sarah assumed she was barren for they had had no children. So she gave to Abraham her Egyptian slave, Hagar, as a concubine. Hagar was impregnated by Abraham, causing the Egyptian woman to become haughty in the presence of her barren mistress. Sarah subsequently treated Hagar in such a harsh fashion that the concubine fled to the desert, only to be discovered there by an angel who encouraged her to return to Abraham's household. The angel announced that she would have a son. Hagar bore this son to Abraham, who called the boy Ishmael. Later, God promised Abraham that Sarah herself would bear his true heir. In a miracle, the ninety-year-old matriach gave birth to a boy, Isaac. When Isaac was weaned, Sarah directed Abraham to remove Hagar and Ishmael from their camp, which the patriarch did only with the heaviest heart. But God took pity on Ishmael and promised Hagar he would be the ancestor of a great nation. Ishmael himself had twelve sons. Biblical scholars have linked these twelve names with twelve Arab tribes, some known explicitly from ancient Near Eastern sources.

According to both koranic and biblical religion, Ishmael is the spiritual ancestor of the Arab peoples of Muslim faith. The prophet Muhammad claimed him as a direct ancestor. While many non-Arabs today adhere to Islam, the faith is Arab in its origins and retains a strong link with Arab culture.

Abraham, however, had a second-born son, Isaac, from whom Jews consider themselves to have descended by way of Isaac's son Jacob. The Bible seems to say that Isaac's progeny are Abraham's true spiritual heirs. As God tells Abraham, "Through Isaac will offspring be considered yours" (Genesis 21:12). Islam, of course, denies this. According to a Muslim tradition (*hadith*), Muhammad boasted of the superiority of his Abrahamic connection: "I resemble Prophet Ibrahim [Abraham] more than any of his offspring does."

What does any of this matter? It might not but for the fact that the personality of Ishmael as the Bible describes him bears an uncanny resemblance to Arab culture in its more dysfunctional aspects.

The question of whether "Ishmael" can be redeemed is really three questions in one. First, it has to be established whether the civilization of Ishmael is dysfunctional in the first place. Is the dysfunction systemic and inherent or does it merely affect a discrete, individual patch of terrorist thinking or fundamentalist radicalism within Islamic culture? To put it another way, is the whole body of the religion sick, or merely a limb or organ?

Second, if we conclude that a systemic moral illness afflicts Muslim religion, from where does this arise? From something in the history of Islam itself, or in the culture that preceded and still animates it? Continuing the medical metaphor, is the condition genetic or acquired?

Third and finally, we can ask if the illness, whatever its nature and etiology, is curable.

So then, to our first question: Is "Ishmael" inherently a violent, angry, resentful civilization, precisely the sort of culture that would be especially prone to using terror as a weapon of first choice? A scholar I know, the University of Washington's Edward Alexander, quips that Islam is the Religion of Perpetual Outrage. Sounds pretty harsh.

Certainly the faith has a violent history. Writes Samuel Huntington, "Some Westerners, including President Bill Clinton, have argued that the West does not have problems with Islam but only with violent Islamist extremists. Fourteen hundred years of history demonstrate otherwise. The relations between Islam and Christianity, both Orthodox and Western, have often been stormy. Each has been the other's Other. The twentieth-century conflict between liberal democracy and Marxist-Leninism is only a fleeting and superficial historical phenomenon compared to the continuing and deeply conflictual relation between Islam and Christianity. At times, peaceful coexistence has prevailed; more of the relation has been one of intense rivalry and of varying degrees of hot war."

There is something uniquely belligerent about Islam. Scripture fittingly reveals evidence of Islamic bellicosity in the figure of Ishmael. When Hagar flees from Sarah, before Ishmael has been conceived, the angel appears to the Egyptian concubine and makes a series of promises about the boy's future: "Behold, you will conceive, and give birth to a son; you shall call his name Ishmael, for the Lord has heard your prayer. And he shall be a wild-ass of a man: his hand against everyone, and everyone's hand against him; and in the face of all his brothers he shall dwell" (Genesis 16:11–12).

The classical medieval rabbinic commentators explained that in the Bible, a "wild-ass" is a symbol of violence, always "searching for [prey] to tear apart" (Job 24:5). Ishmael will be a "wild-ass" in the form of a man. The Spanish sage Rabbi Moses Nachmanides clarified this: "The intent [of the prophecy] was toward his offspring, [foretelling] that they would become great, dwelling in the wilderness like wild asses, and would have wars with all [other] peoples." Another medieval Spanish scholar, Rabbi Abraham Ibn Ezra, said that the phrase "his hand against everyone" meant that Ishmael would conquer many other nations, but "everyone's hand against him" meant he himself would be conquered in the end. Ibn Ezra lived eight centuries before this prophecy was fulfilled with the dismantlement of the Ottoman Empire by the Christian powers that previously had been terrorized by Islamic armies for a millennium.

Interestingly, the Western world's current dysfunctional yet inextricable ties with the Arab world, based on our need for their oil and their need for our money and technology, may also be hinted at in these same verses, according to the ancient and authoritative Aramaic translation of Genesis 16:12. In Hebrew, the angel promises Hagar regarding Ishmael that "his hand [shall be] against everyone, and everyone's hand against him." The translation by Onkelos, a Roman convert to Judaism who lived in the first century C.E., says that the last phrase means, "he will be in need of everyone else and mankind will be in need of him."

Our second question was, *Why* is Ishmael driven to violence? A key text is Genesis 21. It begins with Isaac's birth to Abraham and Sarah, but quickly the focus shifts to Ishmael and Hagar. Sarah observes Ishmael comporting himself in a disturbingly inappropriate fashion, terrorizing Isaac. According to tradition, Ishmael would shoot arrows at his younger brother and then claim that he was only joking. Sarah demands that Abraham eject Ishmael and Hagar from the family. To this, Abraham passionately objects: "The matter greatly distressed Abraham regarding his son" (21:11). But after being reassured by God that listening to Sarah on this is the right thing to do, the patriarch reluctantly complies. The mother and son wander, lost, in the desert of Beersheba. There God hears Ishmael's cry "in his present state" (21:17). In other words, God took note of the youth's righteousness at that moment. Ishmael had repented of his past deeds. Even though God knew that his descendants, the Arabs, would torment Isaac's children, the Jews, He chose to save Ishmael. God sent an angel who promised Hagar, "I will make a great nation of him" (21:18).

Abraham's not perceiving the danger Ishmael posed to Isaac recalls the pre–September 11 refusal by Western leaders to see the threat posed by Islamic fundamentalism. But the primary insight the chapter offers has to do with the origins of Ishmael's anger. Ishmael had expected to be Abraham's heir, inheriting his material wealth and spiritual leadership. The youth's resentment of Isaac, which would only be expected, reminds us of radical Islam's obsessive, hate-filled focus on Isaac's children, the Jews, and their homeland, Israel. Ishmael's shame at being rejected in favor of Isaac recalls the shame at Islamic civilization's failures that drives so many terrorists.

The genealogy of resentment can be traced further back, however. Imagine Hagar's initial pride at first learning that she was pregnant by Abraham, the feeling of being exalted over her mistress, Sarah. Apparently Hagar interpreted Sarah's barrenness as a reflection of some sort of moral inadequacy on the other woman's part. The Bible comments that Abraham "consorted with Hagar and she conceived; and when she saw that she had conceived, her mistress was lowered in her esteem" (16:4). According to tradition, Hagar de-

spised Sarah because it thus became evident—at least to Hagar—
that the mistress was not the righteous woman she pretended to be.
If she were, she would have born Abraham a son herself!

This was followed by Hagar's humiliation at being reminded that
she was still a servant, mistreated by Sarah on whom Hagar looked
down as her moral inferior. The concubine's distress was so great
that she ran away into the emptiness of the desert. Nachmanides sees
Hagar's shame as the very inception of Muslim outrage, especially at
Jews: "Our matriarch Sarah sinned in this oppression [of Hagar], as
did Abraham [sin] in allowing her to do so. God [therefore] 'heard
her prayer' [16:11] and gave her a son who would be 'a wild-ass of a
man,' to oppress the descendants of Abraham and Sarah with all
sorts of oppression." Thus when President Mahmoud Ahmadinejad
of Iran vows to "wipe Israel off the map," he is merely promising to
carry out the ancient revenge inscribed in Ishmael's cultural DNA.

In Islamic society, dishonor is taken with far more seriousness
than in our Western culture. Writes David Pryce-Jones in his study
The Closed Circle: An Interpretation of the Arabs (1989): "Acquisi-
tion of honor, pride, dignity, respect and the converse avoidance of
shame, disgrace, and humiliation are keys to Arab motivation. . . .
What otherwise seems capricious and self-destructive in Arab society is explained by the anxiety to be honored and respected at all
costs, and by whatever means." The backwardness of Islamic culture is a source of great shame to the representatives of a faith that
sees itself as the final, definitive revelation of Godly wisdom to the
world. They seek revenge, against both Christians and Jews.

Now, we turn to the third question posed earlier, the good news. Despite his flaws, Ishmael is a model of repentance and redemption. As
the Talmud shows from a close reading of verses, he ended his days
as a righteous person. This comes out in the Bible's telling of the
events that immediately followed Abraham's death: "And Abraham

expired and died at a good old age, mature and content, and he was gathered to his people. His sons Isaac and Ishmael buried him in the cave of Machpelah, in the field of Ephron the son of Zohar the Hittite, facing Mamre" (Genesis 25:9). When Abraham died, Isaac and Ishmael together buried him with Ishmael giving precedence to Isaac. Evidently, whatever alienation there had been between the two brothers was now past and done with. Ishmael accepted their father's will that Isaac assume spiritual leadership of the family, as indicated by the fact that Isaac's name comes first in the verse quoted above. Abraham apparently was aware of this before he passed away, as we can assume from Scripture's statement that he died "at a good old age, mature and content" (25:8). Would his old age be "good," would he be "content," if his firstborn son, whom he loved, had not come back permanently to the family's bosom?

A rule of classical biblical interpretation holds that the scriptural stories didn't just happen once, never to be repeated. Instead they set patterns that history will follow down to the end of history. In Judaism, this rule is formulated succinctly: "The deeds of the fathers are a sign unto the children."

This is true of Ishmael, representing Islam. His story is one of alienation, jealousy, outrage, and violence—but with repentance, reconciliation, and renewed commitment to the ethical norms of Abrahamic religion at the end. While voices in the media and academia insist with increasing stridency that ideals of democracy and freedom can never be implanted in the Islamic East, biblical tradition insists that Ishmael is redeemable, and that Islam can be turned to the good.

That doesn't mean the United States was right to invade Iraq. It doesn't mean our war will bring freedom to the Iraqis. Napoleon failed, and so may George W. Bush. But at least let it be said that the president's optimism was not without a foundation—an inspiring and uplifting one, found in the Bible.

21

Israel and Zionism: Why I'm Not a Zionist but Christians Should Be

The question of how America relates to Muslims and Arabs is inseparable from how our country relates to the Jewish state in the Middle East. No one could run for the presidency of the United States without at least articulating, even if he doesn't sincerely feel it, an affectionate support for Israel. No doubt, some politicians express such affection verbally while not fully grasping its deeper implications. Thus Barack Obama answered a question from CNN's Soledad O'Brien about his "very clear . . . support of Israel" with a series of less than clear retreats to the passive tense.

"Israelis have been killed. They've got bombs flying into their territories right now," answered Senator Obama. "When your brothers or sisters have been killed in a suicide bombing, when you feel that you've been oppressed or treated unjustly, it's very hard to get out of that immediate anger and seek reconciliation." Notice here the clever refusal to indicate *who* is killing Israelis. The bombs seem to be "flying" of their own free will. People are getting "killed" in suicide bombings, but without any indication of who if anyone is killing them. You might think that to anybody committed to genuine support of the state of Israel, these statements with their hypocritically implied denial of reality would be transparent. Doesn't the political cause of contemporary Zionism include an imperative to see through the pretense of sympathy in ambiguous statements like Obama's? Yet the American Jewish community remains firmly in the pocket of the Democratic Party. What are we to do with this paradox?

Allow me to offer a personal confession. Despite being an Orthodox Jew, I'm not a Zionist. At the same time, and this may seem contradictory, I believe a certain sort of Christian Zionism is appropriate and obligatory. In a biblical-constitutional American nation where Christians are the majority, strong support for the state of Israel would be natural.

Many Israel supporters will call me irresponsible for venturing such a confession. A bitter struggle among pundits and activists has been waged lately around the issue of pro-Israel lobbying. Critics decry the "powerful" (as it is always tiresomely described) American Israel Public Affairs Committee (AIPAC), along with other pro-Israel Jews, for allegedly pressing America to make war on Iraq. According to this paranoid scenario, the war was waged on behalf of Israel.

No, I don't have any major criticism of Israeli treatment of Palestinians, the so-called Israel Lobby, or America's supportive policy toward Israel. AIPAC's critics seem never to grapple with the simple observations that (a) the Bush administration's top echelon includes no Jews, and (b) Jews' communal leaders overwhelmingly and foolishly opposed Bush's election. So the "powerful" American Jewish community has no obvious source of leverage with the president or his top advisers.

Still, Israel partisans will call it irresponsible to do anything other than cheer for the Jewish state and decry her critics. But I disagree, for two reasons. First, Israel has always been vulnerable to criticism and attack and will remain so for the foreseeable future. If this vulnerability is allowed to serve as a damper on truthful discussion, then we will never have a chance for honesty.

Second, if Republicans are Israel's best friends, as thank God they are, that's not because of Jewish leverage. It is because of Christian Zionism in the Evangelical community. Whether Jews see religious significance in the state of Israel won't change how President Bush or his fellow Evangelical Christians feel. So why not be honest about Zionism?

I am not an anti-Zionist but rather, simply, a non-Zionist. The word "Zionism" has more than one meaning. In secular terms, it stands for the belief that Jews deserve a home in the historical land of Israel. That definition is a lot less interesting, however, than the religious spin on the idea. The latter invests a feeling of sanctity not only in the land of Israel, a cardinal principle of Judaism, but in the picture of a Jewish-led state established on top of the land.

Among religiously committed Jews, the debate about religious Zionism goes back to the mid-nineteenth century, decades before secular Zionism was championed by Theodor Herzl. Two influential German Orthodox rabbis held contrasting views. Zvi Hirsch Kalischer (1795–1874) argued in his book *Derishat Tzion* (1862) that Jews could bootstrap themselves into the promised era of redemption, described in the teachings of the Hebrew prophets, by settling the holy land right now and resuming the sacrificial service—offering animals on the sacred altar, as the Torah prescribes.

For centuries before that, Jews had been individually settling in Palestine, returning from the exile imposed on them by the Roman Empire. For example in the sixteenth century, under the rule of the

Ottoman Empire, the thriving Jewish community at Safed initiated an important revival of kabbalistic study and practice. They weren't Zionists. Kalischer's innovation was to call for a mass return of Jews to Israel in the form of a Jewish "colony."

Kalischer's contemporary, Rabbi Samson Raphael Hirsch, whom we have met already, would tell you there is plenty wrong with that idea. In his philosophical summary of Jewish religious practice, *Horeb* (1837), Hirsch seemed to anticipate the emerging mood among his fellow Jews that would ultimately result in full-blown Zionism. Though Hirsch is the godfather of Modern Orthodoxy, his view is associated today, ironically, with the Charedi style of Jewish religious observance, sometimes called "ultra-Orthodox" but more accurately defined by its isolationist posture in relation to the corrupt modern world.

Hirsch's non-Zionism was not driven by a wish to protect Jews from the world but rather by the very opposite impulse. He argued that Jews have a "mission" to humanity. Jews, he explained, are "bearers of an eternal idea, an eternal mission, and of a God-given destiny which, in [the people] Israel, overshadowed, and still overshadows, the existence of a State."

He continued, "But this very vocation obliges us, until God shall call us back to the Holy Land, to live and to work as patriots wherever He has placed us, to collect all the physical, material and spiritual forces and all that is noble in Israel to further the weal of the nations which have given us shelter. It obliges us, further, to allow our longing for the far-off land to express itself only in mourning, in wishing and hoping; and only through the honest fulfillment of all Jewish duties to await the realization of this hope. But it forbids us to strive for the reunion or the possession of the land by any but spiritual means."

This is the apparent meaning of a famous passage in the Talmud (*Ketubot* 111a), interpreting a verse in the Bible's Song of Songs: "I charge you, O daughters of Jerusalem, by the gazelles, and by the hinds of the field, that you stir not up, nor awake my love, till it please" (2:7). The whole lyrical Song of Songs, phrased in the Bible as a conversation between passionate but star-crossed lovers, is traditionally understood as a metaphor describing the relationship between God and the Jews. Rabbi Zeira explains that the Jews are forbidden to "scale the wall," ascending to the holy land en masse and with the use of force, until "it pleases" God. How will we know when this pleases Him? When mass migration to Israel is unopposed by other peoples living there. When will that be? In the time of the Messiah.

To return as a people to Israel in the Messianic era, called by God, when our mission to uplift others had already been accomplished, was the divine plan. To return prematurely would be to abandon the project that God sent us out from our land to accomplish in the first place.

Does this seem to contradict the Bible's promises that God has granted the Jews the land of Israel in perpetuity? Not at all. Certainly there is a Jewish moral right to live in the land. However, this doesn't necessarily translate into a right to rule the land. This is a message of one of the Bible's often overlooked tragic stories, that of Gedaliah, the last Jewish governor of Judah. In 587 B.C.E., Jerusalem and its great Temple were seized and burned by the kingdom of Babylonia. The Babylonian king, Nebuchadnezzar, took the Jewish king, Zedekiah, as a captive and replaced him with a governor, Gedaliah. The latter assured his Jewish brethren, "Settle in the land and serve the king of Babylonia and all will be well for you" (2 Kings 25:24).

Gedaliah was, you might say, a non-Zionist. He saw nothing so essential in Jewish rule of the land of Israel that would justify continuing to resist the might of Nebuchadnezzar. However, a radical nationalist member of the deposed royal family, Ishmael (not to be confused with the much earlier figure of the same name, discussed in the previous chapter), found Gedaliah's submission to Babylonia to be outrageous, worth murdering him over. Ishmael and a group of ten henchman assassinated Gedaliah. The treachery of Ishmael was considered, in the eyes of Jewish sages, to be so morally unacceptable that a perpetual day of mourning and fasting was established, the Fast of Gedaliah, still observed by traditional Jews down to our time each year on the day following the second day of Rosh Hashanah. Referenced somewhat cryptically in the Bible (Zechariah 8:19), it is meant to recall the dangers of the unrestrained Jewish nationalistic impulse.

Today, we can see the foresight of Hirschean non-Zionism in the debate about the Israel Lobby. When religious Jews address fellow Americans in the media or in any public forum, it is rarely with a view to sharing the wisdom of the Hebrew Bible. Instead, the issue is usually Israel, how unfair her critics are, how deserving she is of protection from enemies in her neighborhood, and so on. Jewish and other defenders of Israel are right, in the narrow context of the questions set before them by interviewers on CNN or in *The New York Times*. But it is all a colossal distraction from the purpose God defined for us in sending us into exile two thousand years ago. Hirsch, I think, would say Zionism was a mistake.

Don't get me wrong. I don't fault other Jews for their pro-Israel activism. For better or worse, about half of world Jewry lives in Israel. Obviously, their safety must be deemed a most urgent concern. But what is urgent has a tendency to crowd out what is, from the perspective of eternity, certainly no less important. That is a tragedy.

Practically speaking, there is no going back, no disassembling the state that has been assembled. Israel must be defended. If my son Ezra, when he grows up, were to join the Israeli army, I would be proud. Nevertheless, we should not lose sight of what the state's establishment cost us. In the post-Holocaust era, a time of unprecedented openness in the Christian world to Jews and Jewish wisdom, just when gentiles were ready to begin hearing what we have to say, half of us retreated to a holy sanctuary where we are cut off, largely irrelevant to discussion of how the world's nations should construct their politics and culture, heard, if at all, when we are crying for help.

The reason I am not a Zionist is because religious Zionism, in seeking to import a pedestrian nineteenth-century nationalism into God's eternal Torah, causes us to forget what it is that He has in mind for us. That is, for us as Jews. For Christians it's a different matter, as millions of Evangelicals understand.

Today, if asked why they seek to protect and defend the Jewish state, and more critically why they see this as a religious obligation, thoughtful Evangelicals point to their straightforward reading of biblical verses. They read the Bible from page 1 all the way through. When Christians do this, they find numerous promises made by God to the prophets—on four separate occasions to Abraham alone—about the divine gift to the Jews in the form of the land of Israel. The obvious reading would be that these promises still apply in full force.

This is a departure from some more traditional Christian ways of reading the Bible. For more than a millennium and a half, the basic Christian assumption held that the "Israel" of the Bible, the "children of Abraham," was no longer the Jewish people of flesh and blood but rather the members of the Christian Church. The idea, called "replacement theology," left the biological entity called "the Jews" in little more than a ghost existence, basically irrelevant to the salvation history of mankind and certainly with no claim on the land of Israel.

In Christendom, replacement theology was challenged from the nineteenth century at first by a band of British Protestants, the Plymouth Brethren. They were an earlier manifestation of today's

Evangelical Christianity. They felt that their church had departed from a sincere, straightforward reading of the Bible. Led by a biblical literalist, John Nelson Darby (1800–1882), the Plymouth Brethren movement argued that when the Bible spoke of a Jewish people descended from Abraham and possessing a claim on the real estate of the land of Israel, then Scripture meant what it said. The Church wasn't the Jews. The *Jews* were the Jews.

Darby held that mankind had passed through several distinct periods of religious history—called *dispensations*. His theology is therefore called dispensationalist. In the first phase or dispensation, God interacted with mankind as a whole on the model set by the first man, Adam. In a subsequent dispensation, He interacted with the Jews—who, however, disappointed him by rejecting Jesus as their Messiah. Subsequently, God interacted with the Christian Church, meanwhile putting the Jews and their history on hold. When faithful Christians are all suddenly swept up to Heaven, signaling the approach of Jesus's Second Coming, then the dispensation of the Jews will resume, as all the visions of the Hebrew prophets are finally fulfilled.

The Jews were not rejected by God, according to Darby. Nor was their claim on the land of Israel canceled or displaced by that of the Church.

Darby's theology became very significant when it was taken up by American Christian conservatives, often unkindly dismissed in the media as "fundamentalists," among whom dispensationalism is today the standard understanding of God's present relationship both with the Christian Church and with the Jewish people. These conservatives broke with their liberal brethren primarily over the issue of Darwinism. (Liberals felt that Christian theology could accommodate Darwin's picture of a universe without a designer. Conservatives vehemently disagreed.) From shortly after World War I on,

22

Europe and the Culture War: Another Litmus Test

Now that we have worked our way through a list of political issues ranging from gay marriage to gun control to global warming, you may wonder how realistic an expectation it is to find a biblically correct candidate. Do not despair. It's not essential that the scripturally prescribed politician hold the right view on every subject analyzed in the preceding pages. In fact, it's not necessary for the leader of choice to be conventionally pious at all. I personally found it annoying when a prominent Christian Right leader groused on the radio that Fred Thompson, then testing the waters for a presidential run, isn't "a Christian." As a possible alternative, it may be helpful to suggest an easy litmus test, besides that of abortion. Just probe your preferred candidate for his or her feelings about Europe.

Europe is like one of those pregnancy tests you buy at the drugstore. If a blue strip appears in the window, that's good or bad news, depending on your perspective. If a political leader talks about "restoring America's reputation in the world" (Hillary Clinton) or about how "America must once again be looked up to and respected around the world" (John Edwards), that's code for making Europeans like us again not by changing Europe but by changing America. In the last election, John Kerry boasted of having won the approval of unspecified world leaders, who were rooting for him over President Bush. Again, code for Europe. Sentiments like these indicate, as much as anything else a politician might say, a would-be leader's true feelings about the culture war that engulfs not only Europe but, more important, America. Every issue discussed in this book is an aspect of that struggle, which fundamentally poses the question: Does God have a voice in American politics?

The Bible encourages us to think "civilizationally"—in terms of cultural blocs of nations with enduring characters, each identified with a biblical personage. The Bible sees history teleologically, as having an end point, a goal or purpose. When biblical prophecy glimpses the major historical conflicts to come, Ishmael plays no role at all. That doesn't mean America should turn her attention from terror emanating now from the Arab world. But in the long run, a graver peril may emanate from a seemingly unlikely address: Europe. Just as Muslim civilization is represented in biblical thought by the figure of Ishmael, Europe is also represented by a different, slightly later person from the book of Genesis: Esau, son of the patriarch Isaac.

No, I don't have in mind the Islamicization of that continent through immigration. The second and third generations of Muslim immigrants will secularize—as in fact many already are doing—on what has become the European model of radical secularization, as historian Philip Jenkins notes in his *God's Continent: Christianity, Islam, and Europe's Religious Crisis* (2007). And that is exactly the problem.

✥

Abraham's firstborn son was Ishmael, his second, Isaac. In turn, Isaac had two sons, the twins Jacob and Esau. In their mother, Rebecca's, womb, the boys engaged in a fierce rivalry. They "agitated" within her, as the Bible indicates by using an unexpected Hebrew verb that shares a grammatical root with the verb "to run." They "ran" inside Rebecca, which biblical tradition understands as an allusion to character traits already evident in the boys before they had been born. When Rebecca would pass an academy where God's word was taught and explicated, Jacob would "run" as if to escape from his mother's stomach and rush to the entrance of the holy place. When Rebecca passed an idolatrous temple, on the other hand, Esau would "run" as if to escape and rush to enter the blasphemous place where God's sovereignty is denied (*Genesis Rabbah* 63:6).

At their birth, Jacob and Esau struggled against each other for supremacy, for the status of being recognized as the first, the supreme, sibling. In the end, Esau emerged first, red in complexion and with hair already covering his infant body, with Jacob's tiny hand on his heel, indicating the "younger" boy's dissatisfaction at having lost the race. Tradition understands their wrestling in the womb as a harbinger of a future pattern in history. The Godly culture is always forced to struggle against the un-Godly. When one slips from supremacy, the other immediately takes his place. They cannot rule together, but always eclipse each other fully—Jacob or Esau in the position of chief influence over the world's, or a country's, affairs, never both at once.

Esau was a hunter, an outdoorsman, a rough and violent man, with blood on his hand to match his ruddy complexion. By contrast, Jacob was a "wholesome man, abiding in tents" (Genesis 25:27).

The turning point in their relationship came one day when Esau had returned from the field where had been hunting. Jacob, the homebody, was cooking a stew—for which the exhausted, famished Esau expressed a fevered desire. He begged Jacob, "Pour into me, now, some of that very red stuff for I am exhausted" (25:30), on which the biblical text notes that this explains how Esau acquired his other name, Edom, or "Red," a name to which we shall return. According to the Talmud, the family had been mourning the recent death of the boys' grandfather Abraham. In Esau's impiety—the fact that he had been hunting instead of staying at home to grieve with the family and eat the traditional lentil stew associated with mourning (a lentil is round, suggesting the cycle of life and death)— Jacob saw an opportunity to gain a permanent upper hand.

He demanded, "Sell, as of this day, your birthright to me."

To which Esau replied, "Look, I am going to die, so of what use to me is a birthright?" (25:31–32).

So the deal with transacted. Later, Jacob would receive the blind, elderly Isaac's blessing, confirming his new status—though Isaac had to be tricked into giving it. In a spiritual sense, no longer would Esau be the leading figure in the Abrahamic family. From then on, Jacob, who later acquired the additional name Israel, would be the true "firstborn."

When Esau discovered the ramifications of what he had done to himself, he conceived an eternal hatred of his brother. The rabbis who transmitted the oldest traditions of biblical interpretation understand Esau's hatred to be nothing less than a law of history: "Esau hates Jacob."

That hatred continues to this day, with each of the twins representing opposing forces in history, the Godly and the un-Godly. Their struggle is the most fundamental conflict in human experience, and it will be resolved only in what the Bible presents as the distant future. The shortest book in the Hebrew Bible, the prophecy of Obadiah, twenty-one verses in length, is the briefest condensation of the biblical prophetic view. Esau founded a kingdom, called Edom, whose overthrow will mark the climax of the historical process. Obadiah's vision begins with the words, "Thus said my Lord God concerning Edom" (1:1).

The "book" goes on to describe the ultimate defeat of Edom. "The house of Jacob will be a fire, the house of Joseph a flame, and the house of Esau for straw; and they will ignite them and devour them." In the very end, "The saviors will ascend Mount Zion to judge the Mountain of Esau, and the sovereignty will be the Lord's" (1:18, 21)—the "saviors" here apparently being the future Messianic king and his company. Edom's defeat is thus equated with the revelation of God's kingship. If so, then Edom's rule means just the opposite, the concealment of God's rule. Or to use the modern term, the reign of *secularism*.

Biblical tradition identifies Edom with a particular earthly power in history. The thirty-sixth chapter of Genesis is one of those chapters people tend to skip. The text is devoted to chronicling Esau's descendants, the kings of Edom, of whom the tenth is called Magdiel. In narrow, literalistic historical terms, Magdiel was nothing more than an obscure chieftain of a desert-dwelling tribe that lived to the east of the land of Israel. According to ancient tradition preserved in the midrashic book *Pirke d'Rabbi Eliezer,* however, he is identified with the might and glory of Rome.

Esau or Edom designates Rome, or more broadly, Europe. Not as an ethnic or geographic identity but as a spiritual one. This is alluded to in his name, as the medieval Spanish sage Rabbi Moses Nachmanides suggests. Etymologically, "Magdiel" means to "exalt oneself (*yitgadel*) over God (*El*)." In the vision of Daniel, among the Bible's most fascinatingly cryptic books, the prophet foresees the rise of four kingdoms, the fourth of which is held to be Rome on the basis of a verse that speaks of its king: "This king will do as he pleases, and he will glorify and exalt himself over every god; and he will utter fantastic things against Almighty God" (11:36). Each of the four successive kingdoms would abuse God's people and God's name, but most hateful of all would be this fourth kingdom.

Rome was the enemy of any religion that worshipped Jacob's God two thousand years ago when Pontius Pilate and his henchmen crucified Jesus and, forty years later, when Roman forces burned the great Jerusalem Temple and conquered the holy city of Zion. Rome sent the Jews into an exile that has lasted two millennia so far, while the land of Israel remained under foreign or secular domination, as it does today. As a Jew, I live in what Judaism still calls the Roman Exile.

The roots of modern secularism go back to the fourteenth and fifteenth centuries with the rise of humanism. Like Martin Luther's Protestantism, humanism sought to give Europeans an alternative to official Catholic Christianity. Both tried to recapture a usable past. While Luther looked back to earliest Christianity, before there was a church to speak of, humanist scholars, writers, and artists invoked the ancient Roman heritage of Europe. The historian Jacques Barzun writes in *From Dawn to Decadence,* "For the original Humanists, the ancient classics depicted a civilization that dealt with the affairs of the world in a man-centered way. Those books— poems and plays, histories and biographies, moral and social philosophy—were for the ancients guides to life, important in themselves, rather than subordinate to an overriding scheme that put off human happiness to the day of judgment. The theme of secularism emerges from this outlook." Barzun summarizes: "Humanism as the common possession of the intellectual class meant old Rome."

The original Italian humanists of the fourteenth century were Christians, not atheists. But they inaugurated the "theme of secularism," innocently opening up a way of thinking—about life without God—that confronts us, in full-blown fashion, in modern secular Europe.

Secular Europe seems weakened today not because its commitment to reality without a Divinity is weak—that is stronger than ever, thank you very much—but because birth rates in Western Europe are below replacement levels. But don't worry, Europe will not become extinct. The threat it poses is, in any event, not based on demographic numbers but on ideological infection.

That point emerges from George Weigel's perceptive book *The Cube and the Cathedral: Europe, America, and Politics Without God* (2005). Like Esau, who despised his birthright, European culture has made a decisive break with its Christian heritage. Discontinuity with the continent's religious past is insisted upon. Weigel writes of "the cult of the contemporary," "the cult of the present and the contempt for tradition," the "rupture with the past." Pope John Paul II described this in an Apostolic Exhortation, "Ecclesia in Europa": "A kind of practical agnosticism and religious indifference whereby many Europeans give the impression of living without spiritual roots and somewhat like heirs who have squandered a patrimony entrusted to them by history"—or who have sold it for a bowl of red stew?

When the European Union drafted a constitution for itself in June 2004, the document cited Thucydides and the Enlightenment as the alpha and omega of Europe's cultural heritage but made not one mention of a millennium and a half of Christian history. In the staggeringly verbose text of seventy thousand words, the word "Christian" cannot be found anywhere.

There are many reasons for Americans to worry about the welding together of the European Union, the supranational entity first conceived in 1957 by—interestingly, given what we know about Esau—the Treaty of *Rome*. As Britain's Lord Malcolm Pearson has sought to warn Americans, the EU is only a quasi-democratic entity, with the bulk of its legislation written behind a veil of secrecy by unelected bureaucrats. It is decidedly anti-American in its foreign policy, seeking to take the place of the North Atlantic Treaty Organization, and currently pressing forward with plans for an expanded EU army. Have we already forgotten the powers of hate and violence that flowed from that continent barely six decades ago? It seems prudent to consider that a powerful United States of Europe would endanger American interests abroad.

But also, and more critically, at home. Secularism is a contagion that increasingly imperils the basis of American democracy, namely American religion. In the Cold War, American communists drew confidence and inspiration from the existence of a mighty communist nation, the Soviet Union. So too, American secularists draw confidence and inspiration from Europe.

A powerful faction in American political life would like to see our country Europeanized. God would vote against that faction. The struggle going on today pits traditionalists against secularists. Will tradition prevail, or will it be crushed by liberalism? As always, it's helpful to look at the question from the perspective of history, a history older than Rome. Has such a culture war been fought before? It has, and quite a long time ago: circa 167 B.C.E. Before Rome assailed Israel, Greece did. The story is told in the Apocrypha, included in Catholic but not Jewish or Protestant Bibles, specifically the first and second books of Maccabees. Reading along, you can't help but think of our own time.

The situation was this: Jewish Palestine was in the hands of the Greek kingdom of the Seleucids, headquartered in Syria under the rule of the tyrant Antiochus IV Epiphanes. A Jewish elite in Jerusalem with social-climbing ambitions, wishing to emulate the Greeks with their cosmopolitan culture (Hellenism), arranged to purchase the high priesthood through the good offices of Antiochus. The Hellenist Jason thus became *kohen gadol* (high priest) and immediately began introducing elements of Greek secularism in the fields of athletics and education.

At first, the effects of Hellenism were enjoyed, as the historian Peter Green puts it in his classic work, *Alexander to Actium*, only by "a select club of progressive Hellenizers," a "specially favored cosmopolitan class dedicated to social and political self-advancement," seeking "sociopolitical privilege and status." This Jewish elite exercised in the new Greek gymnasium—naked discus-throwing was the sport of choice. When not sporting in the buff, Jewish priests abandoned their sacerdotal duties and donned the latest Greek fashions. Embarrassed by the traditional ways of their ancestors, the smart set even went so far as to have their circumcisions effaced through a cosmetic surgery.

But Jason was still restrained by the outmoded pieties and finally was replaced by Menelaus as the new high priest. The latter opened Jerusalem's gates to his Greek patron, Antiochus, who sacked the Temple treasury (where poor Jews had their money on deposit). The radicalized party of Menelaus applauded as Antiochus outlawed Judaism altogether. Books of the Torah were burned, circumcision became a capital crime, and a pig was offered on a new pagan altar in the Temple itself. The Hellenizers did everything America's European faction would do but institute gay marriage.

Am I wrong to compare progressives of today with those who sparked the Jewish rebellion 167 years before the common era, a rebellion that Jews to this day recall at Chanukah? Of course it is the victory of the religious fundamentalists, the Maccabees—who defied Antiochus and his pet Jewish progressives with their "liberal polytheism," as Green puts it—that traditional Jews like me celebrate. Actually the comparison is entirely apt. Probing a leader's attitudes about Europe reveals which side of the culture war he is on, the Maccabees' or the Hellenizers'. The parallels are obvious. They also lead to an interesting prediction about how our own culture war will work out.

Then, as now, the conflict pitted secular values (the gymnasium, immodest dress, or lack of dress, and other Greek fashions) against traditional religious values. Then as now, sex was a central issue for the progressives. Why else make such a fuss about circumcision, a mark on the male organ serving the purpose of sobering up the Jewish man when he is about to do something sexually inappropriate?

Then, as now, the progressives were driven as much by social ambition as by principle. For many liberals, one's politics serve as proof that unlike your poor ignorant immigrant grandparents, you get it. You are as sophisticated in your social views as anyone who isn't the grandchild of poor ignorant immigrants. For Jews and Americans of other backgrounds, caught in the web of social anxiety, liberalism is the comforting potion you swig to remind yourself you're as good as your fanciest neighbors.

Where then will it end? The fact that liberalism for many is a function of social ambition and status anxiety happens to be the fatal flaw of progressivism as a political philosophy. Its followers think they are all die-hard believers in the lefty cause, but are they? They weren't in 167 B.C.E., which is why the forces of biblical tradition prevailed.

As Green writes, the conservatives "were stronger, and more numerous, and the more passionate in their beliefs: they stood firm in the face of odds, and were prepared to make sacrifices, indeed to die, for what they held most dear. Even the most energetic and seductive Hellenizing propaganda failed to soften the vast majority of Jerusalem's religious fanatics."

So it was. So it is. And one hopes, with God on our side at the voting booth, so it will be.

23

How God Would Vote

He would vote for political freedom, the system of governance most likely to result in a culture of moral responsibility—the very opposite of the liberal politics of *tumah* that I described in Chapter 2 and have had occasion to invoke in subsequent discussions. The politics of the Bible is the politics of ordered liberty. It is resoundingly conservative.

As concluding witnesses to this idea, from whom I take courage in saying it, allow me to introduce two figures from American history of the previous century: William James and Whittaker Chambers.

Part of my attraction to talking openly about the Bible's politics is that such a discussion represents a direct response to the critique of religion made by the New Atheists to whom I alluded in Chapter 1. In this, I have been influenced by James, the psychologist and philosopher, who died in 1910. William James is not thought of as a religious conservative, nor as an orthodox believer at all. Yet a comforting observation to be drawn from his writing is that America went through a crisis similar to that of today, pitting atheism against theism, more than a century ago. That we emerged intact then may have been thanks partly to insights offered by James.

The defense of religion became a great theme in his work. James the instinctive contrarian lived through Darwinian evolution's earliest acceptance, which he often noted with approval even as he perceived its radical challenge to religion. Darwin's theory claims that a purely material, unguided process alone, with no goal or purpose, fully accounts for the development of life. That would put God out of business. James himself felt "like a man who must set his back against an open door quickly if he does not wish to see it closed and locked." Shrewdly, he noted that in keeping a door open for faith he had more credibility because he was not orthodox—indeed he was irritated by orthodox Christianity—but rather an outside observer. I identify with him.

We can imagine his response to our New Atheists and other militant secularists. Citing God's instruction to the Israelite leader Joshua, "Be strong and of a good courage" (Joshua 1:6), James argued that it is more reasonable to act from the hope that religion is true, than it is to spurn faith out of the fear that it might be false. He appreciated Scripture as a potential "guide to life," the practical effects of whose guidance can be gauged. According to the philosophy called pragmatism that he developed, this is the preferred way to evaluate any truth claim. Pragmatism, he wrote, judges theological ideas by the twofold criteria of whether they mesh with "other truths that also have to be acknowledged," and whether they have "value for concrete life." Do they illuminate the world we live in? Do they include more of reality than rival ideas? Are they borne out by practical experience? If a biblical worldview does a better job of these than the secular alternative, that for James would make religion "true."

Among other contributions, religion provides a framework for diagnosing the ills of a culture, and for prescribing measures for the amelioration of social and political problems. James believed in testing ideas empirically, including religious ideas. In this book I have measured the degree to which the Bible illuminates the American political landscape, providing insight on the construction of the best style of government. On Jamesian pragmatic grounds, a candid look at the Bible's political platform demonstrates what a timelessly useful book Scripture is, whether it is seen as divine revelation or simply as the treasured wisdom of mankind. This is one answer to the New Atheists. Among other reasons for faith, the Bible is true because it sheds more light on public life than secularism does.

No one would understood that better, I think, than one of the most eloquent spokesmen for liberty that the twentieth century produced. More than fifty years ago, Whittaker Chambers wrote his great memoir, *Witness,* about his break with the Communist Party, a story that culminates in his public accusation against a fellow communist, Alger Hiss. Chambers and Hiss were both agents for the Soviet Union, filching American state secrets and delivering them to a Soviet handler. Their espionage ring was centered in Washington, D.C., where Hiss was a high official in the State Department. Chambers, unlike Hiss (as far as we know), became disillusioned with communism, an ideology that he ultimately understood as being merely a mask that another, deeper belief system—secularism— happened to wear for convenience. It was never about economics, really. It was about man and God.

Communism began to unravel and disintegrate in Chambers's mind one morning in the Baltimore apartment he shared with his wife and young daughter. He was feeding his daughter oatmeal, some of the stuff landing on the floor, the rest on her face. As I know from teaching my own children to eat, it's a monotonous process. The monotony was broken by a revelation.

Suddenly, the father's eye was transfixed by the little girl's ear. It was the beauty and the intricacy of it that stunned him. He writes, "My eye came to rest on the delicate convolutions of her ear—those intricate, perfect ears. The thought passed through my mind: 'No, those ears were not created by any chance coming together of atoms in nature (the Communist view). They could have been created only by immense design.' The thought was involuntary and unwanted. I crowded it out of my mind. But I never wholly forgot it or the occasion. I had to crowd it out of my mind. If I had completed it, I should have had to say: Design presupposes God. I did not then know that, at that moment, the finger of God was first laid upon my forehead."

Chambers goes on to explain that there are only two political paths. One defines itself with reference to God. The other with reference to man. In the former, man is seen as possessing a soul. In the latter, not. Chambers summarizes the view offered in my book in two brief sentences. First, "Without the soul, there is no justification for freedom." A human without a soul is little better than an animal, driven by urges beyond his control, a creature of *tumah*. Furthermore, man is a dangerous animal. Those with the power to free him would be well advised not to do so. And so they do not. Communism, in denying man a soul, naturally felt comfortable enslaving its subjects.

Second, writes Chambers, and this follows from what I have just said: "Political freedom, as the Western world has known it, is only a political reading of the Bible." Biblical governance, if practiced according to an authentic reading of Scripture as I've tried to offer in this book, is another way of speaking about ordered liberty.

In the 1940s when Whittaker Chambers was an agent for the Soviet Union, the secular vision of man wore the mask of communism. Today, with the economics of communism having been revealed in all its horror and shame by the collapse of the Soviet Union, secularism wears another mask, that of left liberalism, which in a gruesome irony has found it increasingly useful to express itself in pseudo-religious language. God would vote to resist the sly temptation posed by liberal candidates who use faith as a tool and a disguise to mislead voters.

To affirm that truth in 2008 is a frightening prospect, even in our country with its abiding Judeo-Christian heritage, exposing the person who does so to abuse and condemnation by his "tolerant" secularist neighbors. But America could use more citizens who openly advocate the politics of the Bible rather than fearing to say what they really think.

ACKNOWLEDGMENTS

This book reflects not only my efforts but the support and indulgence of colleagues, friends, and family members. I owe them all much gratitude.

In many ways I owe my writing career itself to Adam Bellow, my editor. He has acquired every one of my five books, each of which he played the key role in helping me to conceive. My agent, Milly Marmur, has also been with me from the start, a source of friendship, encouragement, and good advice.

I'm very fortunate to have found an inspiring circle of friends and colleagues at the Discovery Institute. Under the leadership of Bruce Chapman and Steve Meyer, Discovery has to be America's most daring think tank, taking on issues that conservatives and others shy from and doing so with intelligence and discernment. This book was written under the sponsorship of Discovery's program in Religion, Liberty and Public Life. Bruce Chapman and John West read earlier versions of this book. Of course, nothing I have written in *How Would God Vote?* should be construed as necessarily reflecting the views of the Discovery Institute or anyone who works there apart from myself. Any errors of fact or judgment are my own.

During the time I was finishing the book our twins, Jacob and Saul, were born. Apart from the excitement and amusement they have provided, these two excellent babies posed many logistical challenges to our family, a family that already included their three siblings, all under six years old. Any hope of my completing this project was dependent on the astonishingly gracious and generous help of our dear friends in the Jewish community, to which we are proud to belong. They include Devorah and Rabbi Yechezkel Kornfeld, Diane and Michael Medved, Terry and Dan Schneeweiss, Shelly and Mike Brown, Tami and Marty Rabin, Jody and Rick Negrin, Robin and Yoel Lessing, Bluma and Mike Ekshtut, Barbara Cohen, Sharon Boguch, and Susan and Rabbi Daniel Lapin. Rabbi Lapin, longtime friend and mentor, was the first person to impress on me that biblical religion is relevant to all of life, including politics, not only for Jews but for everyone.

I wish to thank some editors who have published articles in which I first tested my approach to explicating the politics of the Bible, letting me gauge the strength of certain ideas by exposing them to thoughtful readers: J. J. Goldberg and Oren Rawls at the *Forward*; Kathryn Lopez at *National Review Online*; Agnieszka Tennant at *Christianity Today*; Zelda Shluker at *Hadassah*; Alice Chasan at *Beliefnet*; and Joey Kurtzman at *Jewcy*.

Thank you to Daniel Feder, Adam Bellow's able assistant at Doubleday.

As with my last book, I had the pleasure of writing a good portion of this one in the beautiful and scandalously underutilized surroundings of the Seattle Central Library's Eulalie and Carlo Scandiuzzi Writers' Room.

As always, our family was blessed throughout by the amazing generosity of parents and grandparents: Arlene and Paul Kaye, Nina Erastov, and Harriet Waring.

Last but above all by a long measure, my beloved and beautiful wife Nika is a life preserver and life enhancer. She makes everything I do—at least, whatever good there may be in what I do—possible. Someday, our children will testify to that. I love you.

INDEX